On Love

20 Lessons for
the World We Seek

Paul & Janet Chilcote

Abingdon Press

ON LOVE:
20 LESSONS FOR THE WORLD WE SEEK

Copyright © 2025 by Abingdon Press

ISBN: 9781791040079
Library of Congress Control Number: 2025935403

MANUFACTURED IN THE UNITED STATES OF AMERICA

We dedicate this book to our son, Jonathan,
whom we will first meet in heaven.
We give thanks for his short life,
and our grief journey that opened our hearts
to more deeply love those who grieve.

To love is all my wish, I only live for this.
—Charles Wesley

Contents

A Guide for Personal Reflection and Group Discussion, written by the authors, is available as a free download at:

www.abingdonpress.com/on-love-extras

The guide includes a six-week pattern for group discussion as well as a twenty-week pattern for personal study, each including reflection or discussion questions and scripture passages that accompany the material in this book.

Prologue
Love in Action Today

If you question whether love has a place in this dark era of hostility and conflict, we want to shine a beacon of hope on your path. If you fear there may be no antidote to your sense of alienation, fear, and loneliness, we pray you won't shut down quite yet. If you find it increasingly difficult even to talk across the divides that separate us today, we don't want you to give up. If you feel paralyzed in the face of such monumental global and political discord, we want to encourage you to stay on course. If you have a deep hunger for tangible, practical ways to live the way of love in our broken world today, then this book is for you.

We have encountered so many people who are struggling with the practical issues of an authentic life of love. Perhaps you are one of those people. You are looking for something practical, well-grounded, and applicable in the face of so many obstacles. Perhaps you believe, with us, that love is an action, a commitment, a way of life, but you need realistic guidance about do-able ideas you can put into practice in your daily life. You don't need a theological argument; you need and want to practice love in a meaningful and faithful way for a time such as this. You want to know about and to implement loving practices adaptable to everyday life that will make a difference in the world.

These struggles manifest differently for each person. Some find themselves overwhelmed by family conflicts that seem impossible to resolve. Others feel paralyzed by workplace tensions or community divisions. Many wrestle with how to respond to global crises that touch their daily lives. The common thread we've observed is a deep yearning for practical wisdom—not just inspiration, but actual tools and practices that can help navigate these challenges with love.

Here is what we believe. We believe that you can choose to live a loving life. We believe you can live daily and richly in practical ways that make this world more loving and just. We believe it is possible to know more fully what love looks like in the events of an ordinary day. We believe you can adopt the way of love, reminding everyone around you (and yourself) about the central place of goodness, beauty, and love. We believe you can be an active participant in the love that surrounds you each day. We believe that love is not just an emotion but a skill that can be developed, a practice that can be refined, and a way of life that can be cultivated. When we say you can choose to live a loving life, we mean that each day presents multiple opportunities to make this choice—in how you greet your neighbor, respond to conflict, or engage with those who see the world differently than you do. We believe that these daily choices, while seemingly small, accumulate to create profound change. We believe that God is working for good all day long, and you can be a partner in this glorious adventure. We believe you have a place and a role in the rediscovery of the power of love in our time. We believe you have more power to change the world than you think.

The path to living love more fully isn't always straightforward. It requires patience, practice, and often means learning from our missteps. But we've discovered that having a framework—a set of practical guidelines and actionable steps—can make this journey more manageable and meaningful. This is why we've structured this book around twenty essential lessons, each focused on a specific aspect of putting love into action.

In the twenty lessons that follow we identify and clarify some of the key aspects of a life of love. We illustrate these various facets of love's work, drawing on our experiences in life and on stories from a wide range of cultures and communities. We paint a vivid picture of a preferred future into which all of us can live. Love is a constellation of practices, a pattern of living with and before others. Actions, more than anything else, define this way of love. So at the close of each lesson we discuss practical actions you can embody to enhance your growth into deeper experiences and expressions of love.

Accordingly, each lesson revolves around a simple action verb because we've found that transformation happens through concrete actions, not just good intentions. Acts of love, not ideas, change the world. These words provide clues about how and where love happens. Some you know well and use every day. Words like listen, make, fill, find, and walk. Verbs like include, gather, create, promote, and empathize feel more aspirational. Some words like simplify, adopt, plant, and resist imply change. Others like abide, honor, trust, and transform have a spiritual tone. You'll find that some actions feel natural and easy, while others stretch you beyond your comfort zones. All these words align with two essential action verbs—live and love.

Your actions define who you are. Unquestionably, your own quest to put love into action will enrich and enlarge your life. No matter how small, an act of love can have widespread effect. Just imagine the cumulative influence of loving actions rippling through your family, your community, your nation, your world. Mother Teresa has reminded us all that small things done with great love change the world. All this means that you make a difference. Whenever you feel overwhelmed or hopeless, remind yourself that your acts of love can change someone's life and make this world more loving and just. Together, we can do this.

This book presents twenty lessons on how to live a rich and abundant life—the way of love—in a time such as this.

Live to love.

God intends all life to move in the direction of goodness, beauty, and love. You discover your reason for being when you commit to love daily. The practice of love is the key to abundant life.

In a world that often measures success by achievements, possessions, or status, this fundamental truth can get lost: your deepest purpose, your most essential calling, is to love. This isn't just an idealistic notion—it's woven into the very fabric of human existence and flourishing. When people near the end of their lives reflect on what mattered most, they rarely mention career accomplishments or material wealth. Instead, they speak of relationships, of love given and received, of connections made and nurtured.

When we got married fifty years ago, we wanted to inscribe something in our rings. We wanted a perennial reminder of our common purpose in life. We decided on four simple words: *We live to love.* We took the idea from the Bible. "We love because God first loved us" (1 John 4:19 CEB). This choice wasn't just about our marriage—it was about our understanding of what makes life meaningful. Lesson number one: you were created to love. Everything else in life revolves around this claim. The phrase "we live to love" has guided us through both joyful and challenging times. During moments of conflict, it reminded us to choose love over being right. In times of success, it helped us focus on sharing rather than accumulating. When overwhelmed by grief, it prompted us to lean on each other. Through decades of parenting, ministry, and teaching, we've seen how this simple principle can transform not just marriages, but all relationships and communities.

This means you are beloved—cherished beyond measure. Perhaps life has gotten in the way of this deep-down conviction for you. Experiences of rejection, failure, abuse, or loss may have buried this truth beneath layers of doubt and pain. You may not always feel like you are loved, but you are. In this vast universe, you may question whether you have any value or worth, but you do. The simple fact is that you are absolutely unique. There will never be another you—another person with your particular combination of gifts, experiences, and perspectives.

More importantly, you can change this world into a better, more beautiful and loving place. The question is, how do you do this?

The answer begins with recognizing your own belovedness. When you truly understand that you are cherished, it becomes natural to extend that love to others. This doesn't mean you'll always feel confident or worthy—even those who seem most secure have moments of doubt. But it does mean that underneath all the uncertainties and struggles, there's a bedrock truth: you are loved, and you are made for love.

The choices you make do make a difference. They shape the way you live, either opening a pathway for love or creating barriers to it. You can choose to live in love, person by person, action by action, step by step. We don't want to make this sound easier than it is—choosing love often means choosing the harder path, the path that requires more patience, more understanding, more forgiveness. But we are convinced that the practice of love has the power to make the world (even in its brokenness and dysfunction) more loving and just.

Francis de Sales reduced this quest for love to its simplest terms. He said that you learn to speak by speaking, to study by studying, to run by running, to work by working. In the same way, you learn to love by loving. Those who think there is any other path to love deceive themselves. This was his prescription for mastering the art of love, and we like it. Given the fact that love is an action, you can practice it. Defining love in theory helps no one; practicing love helps everyone.

His insight reveals a profound truth about the nature of love: it's not primarily about feeling the right emotions or understanding the right concepts. Love is a skill that develops through practice, much like learning a musical instrument or mastering a craft. Just as a musician must practice scales before playing symphonies, we begin our journey of love with simple acts—a kind word, a moment of attention, a gesture of care. Each small act of love builds our capacity for greater love.

You may have had the privilege of watching children take their first steps. Nobody really gives them any instruction. That first step in their lives is the product of literally thousands upon thousands of observations. Before they walked, they watched. Their own attempts to walk followed all that observation. They wanted to do what they saw, first holding on for dear life to something—anything—because it was scary. That first successful solo step was also the product of countless failures, all of which were learning experiences along the way. Learning to love, like learning to walk, includes modeling and imitation, starting with the simplest actions.

This process mirrors our journey in learning to love. We begin by observing love in action—perhaps in our families, our communities, or in stories that inspire us. We make tentative attempts, sometimes stumbling, sometimes succeeding. Each attempt, whether it ends in apparent failure or success, teaches us something valuable about what love looks like in practice. Just as a child's unsuccessful attempts at walking are actually essential steps toward walking, our imperfect efforts at love are vital parts of learning to love more fully.

God does not despise small things. In fact, God delights in little steps and simple actions. To master the art of love you must commit to live daily and deeply into a fuller love and thereby become an instrument of love in the world. You can be a loving agent of change. Ironically, you will find yourself changed in the process. Little steps can cultivate a limitless love of God. Simple actions can express an unbounded love of everyone and everything else. As we begin this journey with you, we suggest two easy practices right here at the outset that we hope will become spiritual habits.

Firstly, when you wake up every morning, simply remind yourself, "I am a beloved child of God." Let those words—that proclamation—sink deeply into your soul. And as you live through the events of your day, let those words surface anew and define who you are. This isn't just positive thinking; it's about grounding yourself in the fundamental truth of your belovedness, which gives you the security and strength to extend love to others.

Secondly, either through words or through actions, make sure one person each day knows how much you love them. That might be a hug, a word of encouragement, a demonstration of empathy, or an explicit affirmation of how much you value their place in your life. You can extend this practice beyond your circle of family and friends into ever-expanding circles of connectedness. Look for opportunities to show love to those you might normally overlook—the grocery store cashier, the delivery person, the new colleague who seems uncertain. Make these two simple practices your first steps in daring to love more boldly today. Remember that living to love isn't about perfection—it's about intention and practice. Each day brings new opportunities to choose love, to grow in love, and to share love. This is how we fulfill our deepest purpose: we live to love.

Suggested Further Reading:

Mariann Edgar Budde, *Receiving Jesus: The Way of Love* (Church Publishing, 2019).

David N. Field, *Our Purpose Is Love: The Wesleyan Way to Be the Church* (Abingdon Press, 2018).

bell hooks, *All About Love: New Visions* (William Morrow, 2018).

Henry Scougal, *The Life of God in the Soul of Man* (Crossway, 2022).

Children's Book: Eric Carle, *Love from The Very Hungry Caterpillar* (World of Eric Carle, 2015).

Adopt a pattern of life.

Force does not produce a life of love. To become loving means to become your true self, a loving child of God. A pattern of life can help as you seek to grow in love. It is like a trellis that provides guidance for growth in the way of love.

Love does not coerce. Love cannot grow by means of force or demand. Love is more like a flower that emerges and blossoms. This does not mean that work has no place in the quest to live a loving life. But the effort involved takes more the form of releasing than grasping. A flower emerges, opens, and blooms. It doesn't thrust or force its way into the world. If God has made us to love, then loving means discovering your true self. It doesn't mean struggling to be something alien to who you are down deep inside.

Think about how a rosebud opens. You cannot force it to bloom by prying apart its petals—such force only damages the flower. Instead, the bud opens naturally when conditions are right: proper soil, adequate water, sufficient sunlight. Similarly, love flourishes not through forced actions but through creating the right conditions in our lives. This might mean cultivating patience, practicing presence, or making space for genuine connections.

We can't forget, however, that the care of a flower includes a good deal of tending. The environment may impede its growth. Disease sometimes attacks the plant. For a rose bush to prosper you must prune it. In the same way, given the fact that love is contextual and relational, your environment is important. Your life story and your surroundings matter. Unhealthy attitudes, attractions, or addictions create barriers to relationships of love. Loving God and neighbor includes emptying yourself of all those things that stand in the way of love.

Just as a gardener must regularly remove weeds that would choke out beneficial plants, we must be attentive to habits and patterns that might impede love's growth in our lives. These might be obvious barriers like prejudice or anger, or more subtle obstacles like busyness or distraction. The work of pruning—whether in a garden or in our spiritual lives—requires discernment and care. We remove what hinders growth while preserving and nurturing what promotes flourishing.

Love has a greater chance of thriving, therefore, among those who embrace "a long obedience in the same direction," to borrow the title of a well-known Eugene Peterson book. Adopting a pattern of life that includes loving practices is one of the most effective ways to grow in love. Such a pattern is sometimes called a "rule of life." But "rule" in this sense does not mean "law or regulation." We are not talking here about a set of demands to be obeyed compulsively or obsessively. Our experience has taught us that this only frustrates you to no end. The phrase "rule of life" means a guide, a way to live in love. A rule of life sets your course, reminds you about those things that really matter, and fixes your attention on the goal you are pursuing.

A rule of life is like a trellis. We love this image. A trellis is a framework that supports and guides a plant, enabling it to grow in a way that is most helpful to it. As such, rules of life have guided the spiritual life of ordinary people for generations. They are one of the most helpful supports for those seeking to live extraordinarily well.

The simpler a rule of life the better. One of our favorites that comes out of our Methodist heritage is encapsulated in three simple phrases. This rule is easy to remember and provides a template for you to reflect on how you are doing:

Do no harm.
Do good.
Immerse yourself in the practices of love.

These rules help define love in your life. They provide guidance to a question we all ask from time to time, what is the loving thing to do? Like a compass with three clear directions, these principles can orient you in any situation, from the most mundane daily choices to life's greatest challenges.

Think of these three phrases as concentric circles of love in action. "Do no harm" forms the essential foundation—it's where we begin. "Do good" moves us from passive resistance of evil to active engagement with goodness. "Immerse yourself in the practices of love" takes us deeper still, into transformative ways of being in the world.

Do no harm. Every day you undoubtedly witness harmful things. You hear words that harm others. You may be horrified by acts of violence or terror. The ethic of love proclaims boldly, do no harm. Do not participate in evil around you. Resist being pulled into attitudes and actions that demean, marginalize, and dehumanize other people. This isn't just about avoiding obvious forms of harm—it's about developing a sensitive awareness to the subtle ways our actions might impact others. It means considering the ripple effects of our choices, the unintended consequences of our words, the implicit messages in our behavior.

Do good. Every day also provides multiple opportunities for you to do good to and for others. Little acts of kindness send ripples of love into the world. Live with a "pay it forward" attitude. Become more intentional about seeing and trying to understand those around you.

Identify needs. Simply ask yourself the question, how might I make this person's day better?

Immerse yourself in the practices of love. God has promised to meet you in so many different ways. Those places of divine/human encounter are spaces filled with love. God meets you first and foremost in prayer. God becomes living and present to you in sacred texts. God shows up in your camaraderie with other people. God beckons you to embrace love around the Table of the Lord.

God also becomes real for you, as Mother Teresa reminds us, in the distressing disguise of the poor. Love reigns in every act of compassion. Waging peace and challenging injustice lead to a more just and loving world. No act is too small. In all these practices you both embody love and learn how to be more loving.

Adopt a rule of life. Make it simple. Make it your own. Start small. Choose one or two practices to focus on initially. As these become integrated into your life, gradually add others. Let your rule grow with you, always keeping in mind that its purpose is to nurture love—love of God, love of others, love of self, love of creation. Try not to become obsessed with it; rather, let it function as a framework for a life of loving action. Let your rule of life be like a trellis that facilitates your growth in love.

Adopt a pattern of life.

Suggested Further Reading:

Joan Chittister, *Wisdom Distilled from the Daily: Living the Rule of St. Benedict Today* (HarperOne, 2009).

Rueben P. Job, *Three Simple Rules: A Wesleyan Way of Living* (Abingdon Press, 2007).

Stephen Macchia, *Crafting a Rule of Life: An Invitation to the Well-Ordered Way* (InterVarsity Press, 2012).

Marjorie J. Thompson, *Soul Feast: An Invitation to the Christian Spiritual Life*, revd edn (Westminster/John Knox Press, 2015).

Children's Book: Kim Mitzo Thompson and Karen Mitzo Hilderbrand, *I Can Do It* (Twin Sisters, 2020).

Abide in God.

Prayer is all about abiding in God. God is love and to abide in God is to abide in love. In prayer, the mystery who is you engages the mystery who is God. You need time to rest in God and to rediscover daily that you are God's beloved.

Ayoung mother was concerned about her life of prayer. It was nowhere close to where she had hoped it would be. She thought it was shallow and undisciplined. She had three children aged one, three, and four. She poured her love into them every day. She said that in the morning, there was just so much to do to take care of her children. She had no time to begin the day in prayer. She felt like she was failing God. She lived with a deep sense of guilt.

When she came to the end of the day, she was exhausted. She said that she had no energy to engage in devotions or even reflect on her spiritual life. She simply talked to God about her children, her life, her exhaustion. She confessed that she often fell asleep in the middle of those conversations. She said she was overwhelmed with shame. How could she let God down? A deep sense of failure clouded her deep desire for God.

Could there possibly be any more realistic or poignant portrait of true prayer? What a lovely image of falling asleep in the arms of the God of love while trying to pray. Safe. Secure. Enfolded. Loved. Once that young mother realized just how beautiful this image was, she was liberated simply to be. Her guilt and shame melted away as she rested in God.

The most important thing about prayer is not the prayer that is prayed. Prayer is not fundamentally about the discipline, the resource, the tradition, the right form, the eloquence, or the perfection of the art. Prayer is about falling into the arms of your loving Creator. Resting in God. Offering God your authentic self without pretense or fear. Knowing just how much you are loved by this God. Prayer is about abiding in God.

Prayer takes countless forms because human beings are uniquely created. What works for one person may not work for another. Some find God's presence most readily in silence, others in music or movement. Some pray best with words, others without them. Some need structure, others spontaneity. The common thread is not the method but the meeting—the real encounter between the mystery who is you and the mystery who is God.

This young mother discovered that focusing her attention on a work of art, or listening to calming music, or lighting a candle often helped her pray. It shifted her focus away from distractions and random thoughts darting through her mind. Prayer became more like the air she was breathing. Even being more intentional about her own breathing brought her closer to God—the One who breathes life into us all.

Unless you have a deep connection with God—the source of all life and love—you can hardly hope to be a force for love and justice in the world. But if you offer your authentic self to God and abide in God's love, nothing is impossible. This connection becomes the wellspring from which all other loving actions flow. When we're rooted in God's love, we find ourselves naturally more capable of extending that love to others.

At some point in your day spend five or ten minutes in silence with your closest and dearest friend—your loving God. This doesn't need to be a rigid or formal practice. Start where you are, with whatever time you have. Five minutes of genuine presence is worth more than an hour of distracted obligation.

You may find it helpful to identify a focal point of your own, like a candle, or a picture, or a particular place of prayer. If you are an early riser, perhaps you like a cup of coffee or tea in the morning. Even the warmth of that cup can calm you down and promote a receptive spirit. Maybe the end of the day fits better into your daily pattern of life, with the work, the play, the events of life behind you. Or maybe you just need to step out of the day midstream for a moment of quiet in the presence of God. Take a few moments to abide in God each day and ponder how you can translate your peace and love into concrete actions in your world.

Suggested Further Reading:

Patricia D. Brown, *Paths to Prayer: Finding Your Own Way to the Presence of God* (Jossey-Bass, 2003).

Harry Emerson Fosdick, *The Meaning of Prayer* (Association Press, 1915).

Richard J. Foster, *Prayer: Finding the Heart's True Home* (HarperOne, 2002).

Barbara A. Holmes, *Joy Unspeakable: Contemplative Practices of the Black Church*, 2nd edn (Fortress Press, 2017).

Children's Book: Frank Jelenek, *Journey to the Heart: Centering Prayer for Children* (Paraclete Press, 2007).

Find your place
in God's larger story.

Your life is a love story. It may feel like a mystery. To flourish in life you need to locate your own story in the larger story of God's love. One way to do this is to immerse yourself in God's loving narrative as it is told in sacred texts.

Whether you know it or not, your life is a love story. Your journey through life takes you through various chapters, each with its own themes and outcomes. No stories are the same. Your family of origin plays a large role in forming your unique identity. The companions you meet along the way, your unique agonies and ecstasies, the context into which you were born, the communities with which you identify, and the events surrounding you provide the framework for your life's story. Most of us like to think that we create our own destinies, but truth to be told, many forces form and deform our lives.

You may feel like your story is a mystery. Welcome to the club. We imagine that's the way most people feel. If you had complete control over who you are becoming, little mystery would remain. Your story would be a straight line moving ever onward and upward rather than the roller coaster you feel like you're on. But control is a dream, an illusion. In the unfolding of your mystery—your love story—you can only realize the life of love fully as you locate yourself in the larger story of God's love for you and the entire universe.

God tells this grand story of love in sacred scripture. The Bible is a matrix of stories located within God's larger narrative of love. Some of these stories surprise us. Many of those surprises revolve around failure and faithlessness. They report the many ways in which God's people lost touch with the larger story of love. So they come across as supremely unloving and leave us with questions. But others surprise us by the way in which love bursts through. The one constant in this story is that, even when our love fails, God's love is steadfast and everlasting.

One way, therefore, to see how your love story fits into the larger story of God's love is to read the stories of scripture. Ask yourself the question, where does my story fit in? With what stories do I resonate? What stories elicit anger or cause me to question God's love? With whom do I identify, and why? Who are the models of love I seek to emulate in my own life? Scripture does not give us easy answers. Scripture makes us ask the questions that are most important.

Francis de Sales loved scripture. He loved engaging it and developed his own way of immersing himself in the story. This was his way of praying the Word and then living it out in the world. His meditation on scripture became a big part of his own story of love.

This method of meditation upon the Word can be applied to all scripture and sacred texts in other religious traditions as well. Francis preferred focusing on the life of Jesus, because he saw the story of love come to life most fervently there. By often turning your eyes to Jesus, he believed, your whole soul will be filled with his love. More importantly, through this exercise you learn Jesus's ways and form your actions after the pattern of his.

Select a brief passage from whatever sacred texts are meaningful to you. We suggest a story from the Bible— perhaps something from one of the Gospels. Then apply the following steps:

Preparation. Place yourself in the presence of God. Pray for assistance. You might consider praying a prayer like this one: *My God, I place this exercise in your hands. Give me the grace to engage this in a way that is pleasing to you and enlightening to me. I offer back to you all the good I may do as I seek to live into your story of love. Amen.*

Considerations. Read out loud the passage you have selected. Imaginatively visualize the setting of the story you have read and locate yourself in it. What is your role in this drama? Do you immediately identify with a particular person or action? How does this connect with you? Here is a good example. When you read about Jesus calming the storm, don't just analyze the text—place yourself in the boat. Feel the spray of water, hear the howling wind, experience the disciples' fear. Where are you in the story? Are you huddled with the disciples? Standing near Jesus? What emotions arise? How does this story intersect with the storms in your own life? This kind of imaginative engagement helps you discover how ancient stories speak to present realities.

Affections. Identify those images in the story and scene that affect you most deeply. Why do these images, people, words, or actions affect you as they do? What is God saying to you through them?

Resolutions. Convert your feelings and reflections into understanding and then into resolutions. What is God calling you to do in response to your reflections? Are there loving actions that God invites you to consider? How might these actions make your world a more just and loving place?

Integration. Your story matters because it's part of a larger narrative of love unfolding in the world. When you share a meal with someone who is lonely, you're writing a chapter in God's story of hospitality. When you stand up for someone who is marginalized, you're participating in God's story of justice. When you offer forgiveness, you're living out God's story of reconciliation. Each day presents opportunities to align your personal story with God's larger narrative of love transforming the world.

Conclusion. Offer an act of thanksgiving to God for the gift of this time. Pray for God to give you courage to fulfill the resolutions you have made. In all your actions seek to do justly, love mercy, and walk humbly with God. You may want to conclude the meditation with a prayer like this one: *My God, I give you this day. I offer you, with great thanks, all the good I hope to do. Help me to find myself in your great story of love as I partner with you in the good work you are doing. Amen.*

Francis generally carried a word or a phrase from his reflections with him into his day. There was always something that lingered in his heart. He held closely to it for support and encouragement in his acts of love. We invite you to engage in this practice weekly. (Also explore the AP Lectio 365: https://www.24-7prayer.com /resource/lectio-365/.)

Suggested Further Reading:

Teresa Swanstrom Anderson, *Finding Your Place in God's Story: 5 Weeks with the Women in Jesus' Lineage* (NavPress, 2022).

Francis de Sales, *Introduction to the Devout Life* (1609), multiple editions.

Anne Robertson, *What Is the Bible?* (Massachusetts Bible Society, 2014).

Jennifer Tucker, *Present in Prayer: A Guided Invitation to Peace Through Biblical Meditation* (Thomas Nelson, 2024).

Children's Book: Bonnie Rickner Jensen, *God, I Know You're Good* (Tommy Nelson, 2021).

Honor one another
in the family.

Families are the first communities in which we experience love.
When your basic needs are met, you develop a sense of trust—
the foundation of loving relationships. Your love can grow
in the context of your family.

Just as internships with mentors form an important part in the education of doctors as they learn the craft of medicine, the art of loving is best learned by experiencing role models. But unlike medical training, which happens in controlled environments with clear protocols, family love must be learned in the messiness of daily life. Every interaction—from morning routines to bedtime struggles, from celebrations to conflicts—becomes a teaching moment. The home is the earliest school of love, and the effect of modeling by parents, grandparents, babysitters, and extended family cannot be overestimated.

When we started our own family, many people conceived the family as a "nuclear" community of mother, father, and children. Things have changed dramatically since then, or perhaps we just realized that this understanding was too limited. Today we embrace all kinds of families, all shapes and sizes, arrangements and configurations. Whatever your family looks like, we pray you have experienced it as a place of safety, security, and love. But we know that this may not be your story.

All families evolve organically. Your family may be blessed with relationships that are stable, deep, and strong—loving. On the other hand, tensions and dysfunction may have led to division, subtraction, and subsequent addition in your family. Multiplication seems to affect everyone, and that makes all families complicated. Families are amazing and perplexing, enigmatic and inspirational. We wonder if "normal" has ever been a proper description for any family? Not all families are loving; regardless, the family can and ideally should be a place where you learn how to love.

For love to flourish in a family, some unlearning might be necessary. Cycles of violence and dis-ease can be broken, but this often requires the healing of deep wounds. We are not naïve about that. One young woman told us her story. She said that from the time she could remember, her mother said to her repeatedly every day, "You are no damn good." At fifteen she ran away from that abusive home. A dedicated Christian woman took her in and loved her as her own. She helped that young teen rewrite her life's narrative from "you are no damn good" to "you are a beloved child of God." That is what love does.

The family is challenged today as never before. There are no easy solutions to family "problems." We have no magic wand that removes heartache related to abuse. We have no quick fix that restores lost sleep over a child's well-being. In fact, love certainly includes that kind of agony. But we do have some great stories about love in the home that might help you reflect on the following questions. What does love look like in the context of family today? How do you practice love in the home?

A friend of ours once defined parenting as the painful but rewarding commitment to growing up. Parenting involves abandoning some of your own preferences—or selfish desires—for the sake of your children or others in the home. Tough stuff! Parenting requires a monumental shift of perspective as you seek to answer the question, what do my children need most? Try practicing the mantra, "what they need, not what I want." This requires discipline that gets you out of yourself and into those for whom you care—precious gifts of God.

With children there are three key times to show love: upon waking in the morning, immediately after school for school-aged kids, and time before bed. Being fully present (no phones or distractions) and focusing your full attention on the children at those special times tells them they are loved and cherished. Even ten or fifteen minutes means so much to them. Also, never forget that the relationship of the adult caregivers in the family determines the tone of the home—angry or agreeable, critical or encouraging, hostile or friendly. Working on those relationships must always come first. Falling out of love is easy enough; staying in love requires a lot more work, but work that is worth it.

Most families in the past had an inter-generational character. We are quickly losing a sense of connection among the generations. One morning our four-year-old granddaughter came to visit her great grandmother who lives with us in our home. She loves gently combing her white hair. Great Nana smiles at her. They exchange hugs. Through these simple acts our granddaughter is learning to be gentle, patient, and kind to the elderly. This love can also then be extended beyond the home. Take your children or grandchildren along to visit a nursing home. For the residents, seeing a smiling child is a gift of love.

When our girls were young, we encouraged sibling love in several ways. One of our favorite practices was a game we called "Love Surprises." The girls were invited to notice how their sisters' days were going and to look for chances to offer a sibling signs of love. If one had a lot of homework or additional activities after school, one of the girls might secretly do her chores. Perhaps she would clean up her room and leave a note that simply read, "Love Surprise." We were challenged as parents to get in the game as well, setting an example, modeling how caring, kindness, and love brought us joy.

You can also model family love by sharing care and kindness beyond your own home. Our children have favorite memories of "church" from when we volunteered together as overnight hosts, sheltering unhoused families in our Sunday school classrooms. We even helped with the set up that transformed those rooms into bedrooms. They loved "camping out" at church and serving breakfast to our guests. They put their love into action and learned they had a larger family that deserved our care, kindness, and love.

All family life involves shepherding in grace, mercy, and love. Each of us, through simple acts of love and care, leaves a mark on the life of others. As hard as this might be even in the most loving of homes, seek to see your family members as God sees them. Honor one another. Even seek to outdo one another in honor. Grant each the dignity they deserve. Give yourself generously to one another. Look for Christ in each other every day. When all is said and done, you are part of one great family of God's children—a beloved community. We need each other to become fully loving.

Offer a "love surprise" to someone in your family today. If you are distant from one another, consider a phone call or text from out of the blue. Take some action that says clearly and boldly, "I honor you. I would not be who I am without you. I love you." Do whatever it takes to start each day fully present, positive in mood with loving eye contact with your children or spouse. Those few minutes will determine so much. Make it a day where love is the tone.

Suggested Further Reading:

Andrew Billingsley, *Climbing Jacob's Ladder: The Enduring Legacy of African American Families* (Simon & Schuster, 1993).

Pope Francis, *Amoris Laetitia: On Love in the Family* (Our Sunday Visitor, 2016).

MaryJane Pierce Norton, *Your Baby Is for Loving* (Abingdon Press, 2005).

Marjorie J. Thompson, *Family the Forming Center: A Vision of the Role of Family in Spiritual Formation*, revd edn (Upper Room Books, 1998).

Children's Book: Suzanne Lang, *All Kinds of Families* (Random House Studio, 2019).

Gather around tables.

Meals shape us in ways we do not always recognize. You learn how to love as you gather around tables and share food together. All of us are hungry for physical and spiritual nourishment. Eucharist teaches you how to love.

When we arrived in Zimbabwe, a terrible drought had decimated the entire region where we were to live. We soon identified five hundred critically malnourished children in the large commercial farms in the area. Normally they produced food for their entire nation and beyond, but the land was now barren. Every family we visited in the remote rural villages revealed unbelievable levels of deprivation and despair. The scenario was the same everywhere we went.

"Where is your food?" we would ask. "We have no food," came the response. "Only God can save us now." Widows and orphans were most at risk. Whenever we made a delivery of basic food items to those who needed it most, the women would fall on the ground, weeping. Then they would spring to their feet, singing and dancing. We usually took one of our girls out on these deliveries. A physically disabled widow Janet and Anna visited one day had no food, but she did get eggs now and then from her chickens. Once they had restocked her home with basic staples, she scooted across the dirt floor on her mat to Anna and put three eggs—all that she had—into her hands. Our African friends taught us the importance of hospitality, sharing, and the significance of meals.

This experience in Zimbabwe transformed how we understand the connection between food and love. While most of us won't face such extreme circumstances, every shared meal carries the potential for profound connection. When resources are scarce, sharing food becomes an ultimate act of love. When resources are plenty, we often lose sight of the sacred nature of sharing sustenance. Yet in both cases, the table remains a powerful space for practicing love.

Consider your own most meaningful memories of shared meals. Often these aren't the most elaborate feasts but the moments where love was most present—a grandmother teaching you to make her signature dish, a friend bringing soup when you were ill, a celebration where the joy of being together mattered more than what was served. These experiences remind us that every meal carries the potential for meaningful connection.

Meals happen every day. More than 75,000 of them in an average lifespan. That means they provide regular spaces in our lives for nourishment, care, and growth—for the sharing of love. Our problem is that we take them for granted. What could be perennial places of encounter with God and each other simply become perfunctory acts to deal with our hunger. But meals hold within them the opportunity to establish and deepen relationships. Each meal shapes you in one way or another—forms a bond, puts everyone on the same level—makes us one.

Approach meals, therefore, with intentionality. This intentionality can take many forms:

- Create rituals that mark the meal as special, even if simple
- Practice genuine presence by putting away devices and distractions
- Share stories and experiences from the day
- Express gratitude not just for the food but for each person present
- Welcome others who might be alone
- Make space for both conversation and comfortable silence

Even when schedules make regular shared meals challenging, we can find creative ways to make our table gatherings meaningful. A quick breakfast together, a weekend brunch, or an evening snack can become sacred space when approached with loving intention.

Don't let this opportunity to love one another in a very concrete way slip by without a glancing thought.

Approach each meal with the question, how can we experience love in this meal, right now, in this very moment? Returning home after time away, have you ever heard these words? "I've prepared your favorite meal." Just think for a moment about how much love is packed into those few words. Remind yourself as you prepare food and prepare to eat that this is a sacred event. Pray a prayer of gratitude to God, not only for the provision of food, but for the opportunity to learn how to love around the table. Encourage your children and spouse or partner to share their experiences of the day. Listen with your eyes and ears. No cell phones or tablets! Dedicate the meal time as a sacred time together—parents must lead the way.

Should it be any surprise, having talked about meals in this way, that a meal stands at the very heart of our spiritual journey as followers of Jesus? Eucharist, the Lord's Supper, Holy Communion is our family meal. Some call this meal a "feast of love." God reveals God's love to us in it. God fills us with love. God sends us out into a love-starved world to share the love that will not let us go. Through this meal we experience the good news of God's love for us all. This sacred meal teaches us many things that can transform all our shared meals: that any table can become an altar where love is offered and received; that any meal can be an opportunity for celebration; and that everyone is welcome at love's table.

The Lord's Supper reminds us of Jesus's sacrificial love for us. As a memorial the meal reconnects us with the love of God in the crucified Lord who sets us free. The Eucharist is a meal of thanksgiving for all that God has done for us. It is a celebration of the presence of the Risen One in our lives today. Holy Communion is an anticipation of the victory of love in our lives and our world. It propels us into the world to be God's ambassadors of love and reconciliation.

Participation in the sacrament can be such a life-giving, spiritually-nourishing, love-inspiring event of central importance. The meal revolves around four actions. These are directly related to your life:

> First, Jesus takes the bread and cup into his hands. In the same way, he takes your life into his hands because he cherishes you and only wants the best for you.

> Second, Jesus blesses the bread and cup. In the same way, God consecrates and commissions you to be sacred instruments for God's work in the world.

> Third, Jesus breaks the bread. In the same way, God invites you to open your heart, to become vulnerable so you can really help one another.

> Fourth, Jesus gives the bread and cup. In the same way, God invites you to offer your life as a sacrifice of praise, a song of love to God's glory. You are an agent of change in the world.

Gather around tables.

The word *companion* literally means those with whom you share your bread. You need companions in life gathered around your table. If you have a family with whom you regularly eat, approach each meal with intentionality and open your eyes to the presence of God in those you love. If you do not eat together regularly, consider putting more energy into creating those spaces of love. The family that eats together stays together. If you lack companions with whom to share your food, seek them out. Invite a friend to join you for a meal. And celebrate love at Holy Communion as often as you can.

Love will meet you as you gather around all the tables of your life.

Suggested Further Reading:

Nora Gallagher, *The Sacred Meal* (Thomas Nelson, 2010).

Ryan Rush, *Restore the Table: Discovering the Powerful Connections of Meaningful Mealtimes* (Forefront Books, 2024).

William H. Willimon, *Sunday Dinner: The Lord's Supper and the Christian Faith* (Abingdon Press, 1983).

Joyce Ann Zimmerman, *Waiting on the Beloved: The Eucharist as Self-Giving Love* (Liturgy Training Publications, 2024).

Children's Book: Abigail Burle, *Around the Table* (A children's book from belongingco.us. Order from https://belongingco.us/store/around-the-table).

Fill your heart with love.

All of us feel depleted and empty from time to time. Life is not easy. The many challenges in life can leave you feeling completely drained. God pours love into your heart through the presence of the Holy Spirit and the beauty of creation.

The metaphor of the heart as a vessel that can be emptied and filled speaks to a universal human experience. Like a well that needs replenishing, our capacity to love requires regular renewal. This emptiness can manifest in many ways:

- Compassion fatigue in caring professions
- Emotional exhaustion in challenging relationships
- Spiritual dryness in times of stress
- Physical weariness from constant giving
- Mental depletion from ongoing challenges

Understanding these patterns of depletion is the first step toward developing sustainable practices of renewal. The goal isn't to avoid emptiness entirely—giving of ourselves naturally creates space that needs refilling—but to recognize when we need replenishment and know how to receive it.

You cannot love others unless you seek ways to fill your own heart with love. Life teaches us that no one can give what they do not possess. Janet had to navigate a tremendously difficult chaplaincy rotation in a hospital. The experience sometimes left her depleted and drained of emotional energy. At the end of an overnight shift, she felt empty and weary.

Romans 5:5 became an anchor for her in her effort to care for others faithfully: "The love of God has been poured out in our hearts through the Holy Spirit, who has been given to us" (CEB). She realized that when she felt exhausted, she needed God's help. Having been drained, she really needed to be filled. She knew that the Spirit of love was there to do for her what she could not do for herself.

She had the inspiration to begin each shift with the following prayer:

> My heart is open, God.
> Please pour your love into my heart.
> Please overflow me with love
>   that I can pour onto others.
> Thank you for the gift of your unconditional love.
> Amen.

The God of creation has also placed healing and restorative power in the creation. This connection between nature and spiritual renewal isn't merely poetic—it's fundamental to how we're created. Research increasingly shows that time in nature reduces stress hormones in our bodies, restores our capacity for care, and awakens our sense of wonder. If you need to fill your soul or to uplift your weary body or mind, seek out nature. In most places you can find a park or tree-lined street to walk around. Take note of the birds, trees, squirrels, and, if possible, a stream or ocean. Look up at the sky. Feel the breeze and inhale deeply. God has filled the world with beauty to nourish and help you. Leave your screen behind and soak in nature. Give thanks for God's beautiful creation. Janet often did pastoral care conversations while walking on a nature trail with a congregant. The walk probably did them as much good (or more) than the talk.

If you fly a lot, you probably have the boarding pro-tocols down pat. One facet of preparation for the flight has to do with oxygen masks that miraculously drop from the ceiling above. But the flight attendant or the video explain the importance of putting your own mask on before you attempt helping others. Not bad advice about life. If you really want to be the kind of person who shares love freely with others, then you must also be the kind of person who fills your own heart with love as often as you can.

Whenever you feel drained and depleted, pray for the Holy Spirit to pour love into your heart. Make that a regular practice. Whenever you feel empty and spent, take a walk outside. Better still, plan for walks daily or several times a week. Open your heart to the presence of God in creation. Walk humbly with God, absorb the goodness, beauty, and love all around you, then let your cup overflow.

Suggested Further Reading:

Joan Chittister, *Monastery of the Heart* (BlueBridge Books, 2020).

Rabbi Evan Moffic, *Shalom for the Heart: Torah-Inspired Devotions for a Sacred Life* (Abingdon Press, 2017).

Howard Thurman, *Meditations of the Heart* (Beacon Press, 1999).

Dallas Willard, *Renovation of the Heart: Putting on the Character of Christ*, 20th Anniversary Edition (NavPress, 2021).

Children's Book: Jenny Copper, *Heart Full of Love* (Imagine That, 2020).

Walk humbly with God.

Arrogance and pride abound today, but humility provides an antidote to the "me first" distortion of life. The practice of humility places you in a different posture in life. It enables you to lift others up rather than knocking them down.

Arrogance abounds today. Many truly believe that to climb your way to the top you must knock others down. Conquest defines success. A "king-of-the-hill" mentality has moved seamlessly from the playground into the state house. Winning is all that matters. We live in an age of me first, my way first, my race first, my religion first, my nation first. First. First. First.

Should anyone be surprised that hate crime is on the rise. Organizations that promote racial superiority—like the KKK, Proud Boys, Oath Keepers, Patriot Front, and Moms for Liberty—spew hatred in every direction. Personal insults, name-calling, and nastiness fill the airwaves. You must be part of the winning team. These values shape our elections and the movement of people into the corridors of power. A plea for mercy on behalf of those at the bottom evokes screams of anger from those at the top. Relationships disintegrate and society devolves. This is a pretty bleak picture, but it does not need to be like this!

We do not have to live like this. The way of love paints a very different picture of life. There is another way. The decisions you make and the actions you practice can lead to a very different world. A proper sense of humility changes all this radically. Humility is a posture and a practice. Humble people relinquish the need to dominate others or to win. They don't wield their power against others. One sentence summarizes the essence of humility: humble people lift others up; they don't knock others down. And you can practice this.

Humility is often misunderstood as self-deprecation or false modesty. True humility is something far more powerful and liberating. It's:

- The ability to see yourself and others clearly, without inflation or deflation

- The freedom to admit both strengths and weaknesses

- The wisdom to recognize your dependence on others and on God

- The courage to learn from anyone, regardless of their status

- The grace to celebrate others' successes without feeling diminished

Humility doesn't make you smaller—it makes you more real, more authentic, more capable of genuine connection. It creates space for others to be real too. In a world obsessed with image and influence, this kind of authentic presence becomes a radical act of love.

For Thomas à Kempis, author of *The Imitation of Christ*, humility is the key to the life of love. Conversely, pride creates an insurmountable barrier between ourselves and God and others. To put it bluntly, pride defaces the soul. The drive to denigrate others destroys life. An intimate relationship with the God of love, on the other hand, forms a spirit of humility in you. Humility leads to a deeper love of God and others. It changes the world.

Gratitude and humility go hand in hand. When you express gratitude to others, you are demonstrating that relationships mean something—they define who you are. Your genuine appreciation for others, especially those who are different from you (or in the world's metrics below you), sows the seed of humility in your life. You need to express that gratitude often. Whereas pride nurtures hostility, humility cultivates gratitude. Humility breaks down the barriers created by hate and fear.

The virtue of humility can only be shaped in your life through practice. One of the most helpful practices in the formation of a spirit of humility is the prayer of examen. It changes your posture toward others and shifts your perspective. Ignatius of Loyola developed this practice as part of his famous *Spiritual Exercises*. It remains the core of Ignatian spirituality and has stood the test of time. It combines the examination of your conscience and your consciousness of God in your daily life. This practice of examining your life through the lens of humility offers a powerful antidote to the toxic self-absorption of our age. Unlike social media's constant demand for self-promotion, the examen invites you into a different kind of self-reflection—one that focuses not on achievement or appearance, but on love's presence or absence in your daily interactions.

Think of the examen as a loving conversation with God about your day, much like reviewing events with a trusted friend who wants the best for you. This isn't about judgment or shame, but about growing in awareness and love. Often practiced at the close of the day or the week, it includes five movements:

Quiet yourself. The prayer of examen begins with a celebration of life and an expression of thanks to God. Assume the posture of kneeling for this first movement. This puts you in a posture of humility before God. You may want to consider turning a chair around and resting your arms on the chair seat.

Seek illumination. Pray for grace to see yourself clearly, in your humility before God and others, and in your pride. Use a prayer like this one in this movement of the examen: *Lord, teach me where and how to find you in the middle of my life. You always seek to lift up your children. You are at work for good in the world. So open my eyes to see you every day. Amen.*

Examine your life. Review the course of your day or week as if watching a video playback. Allow God to show you concrete instances in which you lifted other people up or knocked others down. Picture each person and how your words and actions impacted their lives either positively or negatively.

Relinquish your brokenness. Review your spiritual health with regards to the virtue of humility, and your need for forgiveness and healing. Pray the words of the Psalmist (139:23-24 NRSVUE): *Search me, O God, and know my heart; test me and know my thoughts. See if there is any wicked way in me, and lead me in the way everlasting.* Pray for forgiveness for those situations in which you failed to lift others up when you had the chance.

Embrace God's grace. Give thanks to God for those circumstances in which you were able to lift other people up, even at great cost to yourself. Express gratitude to God for giving you the strength and courage to act in ways that were humble and kind. Live in the resolve that tomorrow is another day, with fresh opportunities to love and serve.

You may want to close your time of examen with a prayer like this one: *Loving God, help me to model my life*

Walk humbly with God.

after Jesus's life of humility and service to others. Give me the strength and courage to lift other people up rather than knocking them down, for your sake and in your name, I pray. Amen.

Suggested further reading:

Hannah Anderson, *Humble Roots: How Humility Grounds and Nourishes Your Soul* (Moody Publishers, 2016).

Paul W. Chilcote, *The Imitation of Christ: Selections Annotated & Explained* (SkyLight Paths Publications, 2012).

Richard J. Foster, *Learning Humility: A Year of Searching for a Vanishing Virtue* (InterVarsity Press, 2022).

Henri J. M. Nouwen, *The Way of the Heart: Connecting with God Through Prayer, Wisdom, and Silence* (Ballantine Books, 2003).

Children's Book: Mary Nhin, *Humble Ninja: A Children's Book About Developing Humility* (Grow Grit Press, 2021).

Make eye contact.

Eye contact feeds the soul. When you withhold eye contact from people, they feel like they have little worth or value. But making eye contact communicates your full attention, presence, and love. It makes other people feel valued.

We love the way people greet one another in African cultures. The Zulu greeting among Southern Africans is particularly meaningful. The exchange begins with the word *sawubona*, which literally means "I see you." The Zulu-speaking people would say that the greeting means so much more than those three English words. It means I see the whole you. I see your agony and your ecstasy. I see your strengths and weaknesses, your passion and your pain. I see your humanity. It means I hold you in high esteem.

The response—*shiboka*—is equally telling. It literally means "I exist for you." Both the greeting and the response establish a deep bond. Both signify the centrality of relationships between and among people. This exchange communicates to both persons just how important they are to each other. These words, and the gestures that accompany them, signal genuine mutuality and respect. They illustrate John Mbiti's insight that, in most African cultures, "I am because we are."

In stark contrast to the Western dictum, "I think, therefore I am," this greeting shifts the focus from "me" to "us" and our essential bond. It elevates the dignity, worth, and value of every human being. A simple exchange on the street reinforces the idea that when someone sees me, I come into being—I exist.

All this implies eye contact. In some Asian cultures, prolonged eye contact may be considered aggressive or disrespectful, particularly between people of different social status. Many Indigenous American cultures teach that lowering one's eyes can be a sign of respect. Middle Eastern cultures often have complex codes about eye contact between genders. Yet beneath these variations lies a universal human truth: the way we see and are seen profoundly affects our sense of worth and connection.

Understanding these cultural nuances doesn't diminish the importance of eye contact—rather, it enriches our appreciation for the many ways humans communicate value and respect. The key is learning to express acknowledgment and honor in ways that resonate within each cultural context. Whether through direct gaze, respectful glances, or other forms of attention, the essential message remains: "I recognize your humanity. I honor your presence. You matter." Whenever you connect with someone in this way, you say, "I see you." Even a person who is blind is not blind to the presence of the other. When you are truly seen you feel like you matter. Nothing could be more important in your daily life, to receive and offer connection. All of us yearn to be seen. We long to be recognized and affirmed.

If you have spent any time around young children, you will immediately note the attention they give to your eyes. It is as though they are panning to identify anyone who sees them. As soon as they locate your pair of potentially empathetic eyes, they will not let you go.

When we were young parents, we discovered the work of Dr. Ross Campbell. The first of his books we read together was *How to Really Love Your Child*. We learned that nothing communicates how much you love someone more effectively than giving that person your full attention and presence. And nothing does this better than eye contact and your focused attention. If you want a small child to "come to life," just look deeply and lovingly into their eyes.

What stands in the way of eye contact and its power to connect us all lovingly? Number one on the list—screens. How many times have you seen a group of people with everyone fixated on their own phone. Nothing impedes human connection more than our devices. Parents seem to fall prey quite easily to this trap. Just go to a park and observe children look to their parent or caregiver to see if they are watching. Climbing or swinging, they look back only to see that special person focused on their phone. Their disappointment is obvious. It's heartbreaking. Children learn very quickly if a phone is more important than they are to their parents. Eyes fixated on a phone scream, "you are less important to me than this thing." So, the child feels devalued, even worthless—not loved.

Given the fact that your eyes speak volumes, you must be careful about what they are saying if you want to communicate love effectively. Eye contact can be very harmful if it is consistently angry. Sometimes when we're frustrated or triggered, we say, "look at me when I talk to you." In that moment, it's important to ask, "What are my eyes saying?" If the answer to that question is frequently anger, then there may be deeper questions you need to ask of yourself. Regardless, ask yourself these questions continually: "Right now, what are my eyes saying to this child, my spouse, my friend, this person I do not know? Are my eyes angry or loving? Do my eyes say, 'You are an annoyance or you are beloved?'"

Another issue. Unfortunately, most of us are programmed to avoid making eye contact, especially with people we don't know. Some of this is cultural, of course, complex and highly nuanced. When our interactions cross cultures and boundaries, it's important to be thoughtful about what we do with our eyes. Eyes give us clues to feelings, vulnerability, power differential, status, and desire for connection. But every day you have opportunities to look upon others lovingly, just walking down the street, at the grocery store, even in your home with those most close to you in life.

With all this in mind, remember that intentionally withholding eye contact can harm others. It creates distance and constructs barriers. Test yourself in this. When and why do you not want to connect with someone by looking into their eyes? What has happened in your relationship that makes you feel this way? Remember that loving, caring, compassionate eye contact can turn this around. Take the initiative to reconnect.

Developing meaningful eye contact in today's world requires intentional practice:

In family settings:

- Create device-free zones and times

- Get down to children's eye level when they speak

- Practice "eye-to-eye" conversations at meals

- Make morning greetings and evening goodbyes face-to-face

- Look up from tasks when family members enter the room

In professional contexts:

- Close your laptop during one-on-one conversations
- Practice engaged listening with colleagues
- Acknowledge people passing in hallways
- Give full attention during meetings
- Make eye contact during presentations

In public spaces:

- Notice service workers and acknowledge their presence
- Share a genuine smile with strangers when appropriate
- Look people in the eye when saying thank you
- Practice seeing those others might overlook
- Remain aware of cultural and social boundaries

The goal isn't perfect execution but gradual growth in authentic presence and connection.

Make eye contact with others. Practice this regularly. Make it a habit. It may feel awkward to you at times, but positive eye contact communicates love. It is a simple act. It makes the other person feel loved. You will soon discover that love grows in you whenever you offer this gift to others. Eyes communicate more effectively, and at a deeper level, than words. Eye contact has the power to change lives—to change your world.

Suggested Further Reading:

D. Ross Campbell, *How to Really Love Your Child* (David C. Cook, 2015) and *How to Really Love Your Teen* (David C. Cook, 2015).

Amberly Neese, *The Friendship Initiative: 31 Days of Loving and Connecting Like Jesus* (Abingdon Press, 2021).

Priya Parker, *The Art of Gathering: How We Meet and Why It Matters* (Riverhead Books, 2020).

Richard Rohr, *Just This: Prompts and Practices for Contemplation* (SPCK, 2018).

Children's Book: Patricia Bardina, *Jovi Giraffe Learns to Look: A Lesson in Eye Contact* (Gatekeeper Press, 2019).

Listen more; talk less.

Listening is one the most important acts of love. Everyone can do it. When you feel heard, you feel loved. Active listening is an intentional form of listening rooted in the desire to embrace and truly understand another person.

Have you ever been in a situation in which you felt you had something important to say? But when you spoke, no one seemed to listen. Yeah, they heard the words you said, but they really didn't listen. You put a large investment into your contribution to the conversation, but no one seemed to care. They brushed off your words, your idea, your perspective. That hurts. There are two things that all of us desire, perhaps more than anything else, to be known and to be heard.

Flip that scenario around and it translates into an extremely important lesson in life. Listening is far more important than speaking. We need to listen more and talk less. Radical attentiveness builds relationships of trust and love. The art of listening is really the art of loving. When someone really feels heard, they feel loved. Listening is one of the most important acts of love. But you must listen with the heart and mind as well as the ears.

Children know intuitively when you are not listening. It's so easy to be in your own head or heart rather than giving them the attention they need and deserve. Regardless, you know when you are not truly present. You are somewhere else. In your own thoughts. Focused on your own tasks or issues. A girl wanted to tell her father something important. He was working on the computer. As she sought relentlessly to get his attention, he continued to type, giving periodic nods with occasional "uh-huhs," "yeahs." Eventually she yelled, "Dad, listen to me!" Impatiently, he barked back, "I am listening!" She retorted, "But your face isn't."

Listening is far more than not talking. When listening to children it helps to sit quietly coloring pictures. When listening to teens it might help to walk together where they feel freer and less on the spot. Art therapy uses this approach, allowing a child or adult to create art and then tell the listener their story. These actions say, "You are worth my time. Your words are important to me. I really do care about what you have to say." We have found that people everywhere are hungry for a listener. Once on a vacation, sitting by a hot tub, a total stranger shared her deepest feelings and life story, prompted by merely a kind smile and eye contact. People long for a sympathetic ear.

Taizé is a unique monastic community in France. Young people flock by the thousands to this community to find hope. The brothers of Taizé have made listening the keystone of their common life. Each day they dedicate time simply to listen to the pilgrims. They ask them about their stories. They invite them to share their dreams. The listening of the monks—practicing attentiveness, awareness, or mindfulness—gives life to these young people. It enables them to blossom.

Listening, like prayer, begins in silence. Total, undistracted silence trains you to listen. You can't hear the voice of God or anyone else unless you are quiet. Silence also permits your mind to surface insights. To listen, you must first be able to confront and reflect on your own fears, feelings, and memories. If you are always talking, you can hold all these deeper parts of yourself at bay. If you can't be silent when you're alone, you can't listen to others in a truly loving way.

According to the renowned psychologist, Carl Rogers, for listening to be an act of love you must be present, active, and focused. Active listening requires intentionality. It doesn't just happen. It's about being fully present, actively processing, and seeking to understand another human being. Each of those components is important: presence, process, perspective.

Deep listening demands that you get out of yourself. It is a discipline of self-control and selfless love. One danger we all face is thinking that sharing your own experience of a situation or problem (often a worse one) shows the other person that you "understand" and thus empathize. Rather, this turns the attention away from listening to *them* and points the spotlight on *you*. True, deep listening avoids "hijacking the story" of your conversation partner. At all costs avoid saying, "I know just how you feel!" Listening requires genuine interest in the person with whom you're speaking, their unique life and story.

It helps to think of yourself as an explorer, entering a new place and wanting to understand the culture and people. Ask open-ended questions rather than making statements. Paraphrase what you have heard to be sure you've heard their message. Listen to understand rather than to respond. Clear your mind of what you want to say. Do not interrupt. Withhold judgment. Avoid giving advice. Receive and accept not only the words you hear but the feelings behind them.

Commit yourself to the practice of active listening every day. Be particularly intentional in your listening with people who are seeking to share themselves deeply or are in times of grief, crisis, or confusion. Be respectful. A good question might be, "Would you be willing to share with me what it feels like to be you today?" Or, "What is going on in your world?" Remember that you are entering someone else's holy, vulnerable space as a guest. Humble, kind listening opens the door. Your active listening can help them know and feel they are loved.

Listen more; talk less.

Practice the following elements in particular:

- Intentional focused presence
- Deep personal engagement
- Thoughtful responsive paraphrasing
- Non-interruptive, non-judgmental understanding

Listen with your ears. Listen with your heart. Listen with your face. Listen as an act of love.

Suggester Further Reading:

Thich Nhat Hanh, *How to Listen* (Parallax Press, 2024).

Emma J. Justes, *Hearing Beyond the Words* (Abingdon Press, 2006).

Carl E. Rogers and Richard E. Farson, *Active Listening* (Martino Pub., 2015).

Heather R. Younger, *The Art of Active Listening* (Berrett-Koehler Publishers, 2023).

Children's Book: Gabi Garcia, *Listening with My Heart: A story of kindness and self-compassion* (Skinned Knee Publishing, 2017).

Empathize with others.

In many of our cultures we seem to be losing the ability to empathize with others. But empathy is one of the most important ways to communicate your love. Empathy—a practice of deep understanding and care—can be learned.

Empathy seems to be in increasingly short supply. Empathy has to do with the ability to understand the feelings, thoughts, and experiences of another person. It entails getting outside yourself and entering as fully as possible into someone else's skin. It involves the whole of who you are—heart, mind, and will. To be empathetic means to enter the pain and joy, suffering and celebration of someone else. Empathy is about feelings, sensitivity, and deep understanding. Without empathy there can be no love and without love there can be no empathy. How unbelievably disheartening it is when best-selling "hard-right Christian" authors publish books with titles like *Toxic Empathy* and *The Sin of Empathy*. But this is where we are today.

The decline in empathy we're witnessing has ripple effects that touch every aspect of society. We see it in the growing chasms between different groups, in the fraying of family bonds, in the tensions that pervade workplaces, and in the rising tide of loneliness and isolation. Each instance of failed empathy creates another small crack in our social fabric.

Yet empathy isn't simply an emotional response that we either have or lack. It's more like a muscle that can be developed through conscious practice. This development happens across multiple dimensions: in our ability to understand others' perspectives intellectually, in our capacity to resonate with others' feelings emotionally, and in our willingness to move from understanding to supportive action.

When we begin to see empathy as a skill rather than just a feeling, new possibilities open up. Even across significant differences—political, cultural, generational—we can grow in our ability to understand and connect with others. This growth rarely feels comfortable. It often requires us to venture beyond familiar emotional territory, to sit with discomfort, to acknowledge perspectives that challenge our own. But this very discomfort often signals that we're expanding our capacity for understanding and connection.

Some people may seem to feel deeply for others naturally. Whether in your nature or not, however, you can learn to be empathetic. We believe that everyone needs empathy to flourish. Like so many other aspects of life, growing in empathy does not go against the grain of how you were made. You are created for empathy because you are designed to love. To grow in empathy often means to strip away—to unlearn—attitudes and behaviors that focus on self rather than others.

In 1996, Canadian educator and social entrepreneur Mary Gordon developed a classroom program called Roots of Empathy. Her goal was to nurture empathy and social/emotional intelligence in children. She felt this would be the best way to reduce bullying, aggression, and other antisocial behavior while promoting peace, one child at a time. This mode of learning centers around the monthly visit of a baby and nurturing parent to the classroom through the course of a year. The children are encouraged to observe and interact, and engage in guided discussions about things like temperament, development, care, and feelings:

> Through the Roots of Empathy baby's first year of life, children are inhaling the social environment of relationship-building, not through dependence on instruction, but through the intrinsic learning experiences of a continuing connection. Values are communicated, and attitudes are internalized. . . . We can only expect children to be empathetic if they've had real and repeated experiences of empathy in their daily lives. Roots of Empathy opens a door to this world. For some children, who have ingested empathy with their mothers' breast milk, it is a familiar world; for other children, whose early circumstances have been less fortunate, it is a world they can feel welcome in and begin to own. (*Roots of Empathy*, 42–43)

Fourteen-year-old Darren's life story was chilling. He had an extremely traumatic early childhood and had spent a decade in foster homes. He was a tough kid. Darren's eighth-grade class had been interacting with baby Evan who was six-months-old when they had a session on temperament. Evan's mother told the class that he liked to face outward when he was in his Snugli. He didn't seem to like cuddling into her. When the class ended, she asked if any of the students wanted to try the Snugli. To everyone's surprise, Darren offered to try. He also wanted to put Evan in and gently positioned Evan facing him. The baby snuggled right in. Darren rocked him in a quiet corner for some time. When he returned to the mother and teacher, he asked, "If nobody has ever loved you, do you think you could still be a good father?" Mary Gordon reflects:

> This boy, who has seen things no child should see, whose young life has been marked by abandonment, who has struggled to the age of fourteen with scarcely a memory of love, has seen a glimmer of hope. Through these moments of contact with the uncritical affection of the baby, an adolescent boy has caught an image of himself as a parent that runs counter to his loveless childhood. (*Roots of Empathy*, 6)

The 24/7 role of parents and caregivers in modeling empathy is so critical. You nurture empathy in children by consistently and sympathetically listening and helping children reflect on and understand their own feelings. This practice, in and of itself, helps you avoid rushing to judge behavior unthoughtfully. Instead of applying threats, bribes, or punishments, that may be counterproductive in the end, empathy opens the door to understanding for everyone. Children who experience empathetic responses to their frustrations and problems, rather than punitive actions, grow up to be empathetic people.

Janet helped launch Family Promise in several communities in which she served. This organization cares for families that are unhoused by providing housing in churches, synagogues, and mosques. It is an amazing program of empathy and love, a tangible expression of God's shalom as families experience compassion and nonjudgmental love. Janet enjoys spending time listening and playing with the children who come as guests. One day she sat for an hour on the floor playing and laughing with a four-year-old whose mother was busy with her baby. When Janet had to go, her little friend looked intently into her eyes and asked what her name was again. Janet reminded her. The little girl smiled and said with deep feeling, "I will remember that name forever."

Whenever you share life with someone in a way that says I really understand you, I care, and I'm here for you, the miracle of connection happens. Love builds an emotional bond between you and that other person. Words that you really mean demonstrate your empathy. "I can see you are really upset." "It must be so hard for you right now." "I am so, so sorry." Questions can also open a window to deeper understanding. "What can I do to be helpful?" "What has this been like for you?" "Are you feeling lonely today?"

Cultivating empathy in daily life involves a delicate dance between awareness, understanding, and action. It begins with paying attention—noticing the subtle signs that signal others' emotional states, catching the unspoken messages conveyed through tone and gesture, recognizing your own emotional reactions to others. This awareness creates the foundation for deeper understanding.

From this foundation of awareness, you can move toward genuine understanding. This might mean imaginatively entering into another's experience, learning about different cultural perspectives, or simply sitting with someone's story without rushing to judgment or advice. Understanding doesn't require you to agree with everyone's choices or perspectives, but it does ask you to acknowledge the complex humanity of each person you encounter.

Yet awareness and understanding alone aren't enough. Empathy calls us to action—not necessarily to fix others' problems, but to respond with appropriate care and support. Sometimes this means standing with someone in their difficulty, working to change unjust systems, or creating more inclusive spaces. Often, the most empathetic action is simply being fully present with someone, offering the gift of your undivided attention and genuine concern.

Here are some questions for yourself at the end of the day to check your empathy meter. Did I express empathy to anyone today? How did I get out of myself to better understand the life of that person? What did I do specifically to help that person know I cared and understood? Do an empathy inventory. Empathy communicates love more effectively to another human being than just about any other action. Share your love freely and extravagantly.

Suggested Further Reading:

Kathleen A. Brehony, *Ordinary Grace: Lessons from Those Who Help Others in Extraordinary Ways* (Riverhead Books, 2000).

Toinette Eugene and James Newton Poling, *Balm for Gilead: Pastoral Care for African American Families Experiencing Abuse* (Abingdon Press, 1998).

Mary Gordon, *Roots of Empathy: Changing the World Child by Child* (The Experiment, 2009).

Becca Stevens, *The Gift of Compassion: A Guide to Helping Those Who Grieve* (Abingdon Press, 2012).

Children's book: Kaitlin Johnstone and Felicity LeFevre, *Kindness Is: A story of true kindness rooted in love, empathy, compassion, inclusion, & justice* (Kind Cotton, 2024).

Resist evil, injustice, and oppression.

The forces of evil, injustice, and oppression are always at work in the world. They obstruct and impede the good life that God intends for all people. Despite the apparent power of evil, love and justice will prevail.

The Prophet Amos provides a remarkably simple recipe for life: "Hate evil, love good" (5:15 CEB). The prophetic witness of virtually all religious traditions calls for a commitment to three critical actions. All three are inseparable from the restoration of love in a broken world. Renounce the spiritual forces of wickedness. Reject the evil powers of this world. Resist evil, injustice, and oppression.

Evil is not merely an idea. Injustice and oppression are not simply attitudes. You know this all too well. People embody these forces antithetical to love in real actions that hurt and harm. Love calls us to action. It demands that we counter-act the influence of these terrorizing agents in the world. Three action verbs describe the necessary response to the evil that surrounds you. Renounce. Reject. Resist.

You already know how evil works. Those who engage in its vicious activities thrive on creating fear, chaos, and destruction. When the shadow of these three diabolical forces falls on you, it stops you in your tracks. And that is the purpose. Fear paralyzes you. Chaos disorients you. Destruction steals your hope. The resurgence of authoritarianism, nationalism or nativism, and racism in our time demonstrates just how powerful these forces can be. There is nothing new in this. But evil continues to surface today in particularly ugly ways.

This means you are called to witness against evil in all its forms. You are called to dispute the validity of authoritarianism and advance the cause of self-determination for all people. You are called to defy White Christian nationalism and advocate the beauty and strength of ethnic diversity. You are called to embrace an anti-racist posture to dismantle racism in all its forms. You are called to counter inequality and discrimination with actions that affirm the dignity and worth of every human being. You are called to work for restorative justice and to fight systems that perpetuate hate. You are called to speak out against the irresponsible use of the earth's resources and the destruction of our earthly home. You are called to oppose war and wage peace with justice. That's a tall order!

Steve Biko founded the Black consciousness movement and popularized the idea that Black is beautiful. He was tireless in his struggle to dismantle the racist Apartheid regime in South Africa and paid for it with his life. Most of us ask the question at some point, "What can one person do?" *The Power of One*, a feature length film that tells the story of Biko's life and death, demonstrates the effect that one person can have to change the world. Nelson Mandela said that he was the spark that lit a fire for justice across South Africa.

The question "What can one person do?" often paralyzes us in the face of seemingly insurmountable evils. Yet history shows us that transformation frequently begins with individual acts of loving resistance. Rosa Parks's refusal to move to the back of the bus, Dietrich Bonhoeffer's stand against Nazi ideology, Dorothy Day's commitment to the poor—these individual actions created ripples that grew into waves of change.

You may say, "Yes. But I'm not a Steve Biko." True. You may not have to give your life for the cause of love, but there is so much you can do. Resistance to evil often begins in small, daily choices: refusing to laugh at dehumanizing jokes, speaking up when someone is marginalized, making purchasing decisions that don't support exploitative systems, creating inclusive spaces in our spheres of influence. These seemingly small acts of resistance, multiplied across many lives, create the conditions for larger systemic change.

Talk to those around you whom you trust. Do something. Take one step at a time. Those who perpetrate evil seek to deter, demoralize, and create the impression of inevitability. But evil is not inevitable. Realize that when you stand for love and justice you are not alone.

Most importantly, use your voice in the service of goodness, beauty, and love. Walter Brueggemann reminds us that you need courage to interrupt silence. Given the face of evil, injustice, and oppression in our world (and your neighborhood), silence is not an option. Love demands that you renounce, reject, and resist these forces that erode love in the world. It requires that you work tirelessly and lovingly for justice. Love compels you to stand alongside the oppressed and fight for their dignity, rights, and worth.

Resisting evil, injustice, and oppression requires not just courage but sustainability. The temptation is to burn hot with righteous anger until we burn out, leaving the work of resistance unfinished. Love-based resistance takes a different approach. It recognizes that transformation is usually gradual, that we need to pace ourselves for the long journey, that we must tend to our own spiritual and emotional well-being even as we work for change.

This sustainable resistance involves building communities of support, celebrating small victories, learning from setbacks, and maintaining practices that nurture hope. It means grounding our resistance in love rather than hate, seeking to transform systems while maintaining compassion for individuals caught within them. Most importantly, it means remembering that we resist not just because we oppose evil, but because we believe in the possibility of good—in the triumph of love over fear, justice over oppression, community over division.

Here are some practical actions, simple steps you can take in this contest between love and evil. We have drawn them, in part, from the antiracism work of Ibram Kendi.

- Pay attention to the voices of people who are the victims of oppression and injustice around you.

- Call out hate speech, name-calling, and bullying whenever you witness it.

- Remind yourself that prejudice, bigotry, and hate are not innate, but learned.

- Model for others your friendships with people of different races and religions.

- Take your family to eat at ethnic restaurants and learn about other cultures.

- If you have children, teach them about kindness, fairness, and human rights.

- Let others see you standing up for justice and standing alongside the oppressed.

Resist evil, injustice, and oppression.

Read Romans 12:9-21 each day for a week. Then strive to live this vision of love in your daily life.

Suggested Further Reading:

Walter Brueggemann, *Interrupting Silence: God's Command to Speak Out* (Westminster/John Knox Press, 2018).

Martin Luther King, Jr., *Strength to Love* (Fortress Press, 2010).

Ibram X. Kendi, *How to Be an Antiracist* (One World, 2023).

Mai-Anh Le Tran, *Reset the Heart: Unlearning Violence, Re-learning Hope* (Abingdon Press, 2017).

Malala Yousafzai, *I Am Malala: How One Girl Stood Up for Education and Changed the World* (Little, Brown Books, 2016).

Transform hostility into hospitality.

Fear often leads to hostility that creates an "us vs. them mentality"
antithetical to love. Hostility builds walls between people. But
hospitality has the power to break down walls, soften hearts,
and establish relationships of love.

We live in an age of hostility. Life is never easy in this kind of world. Polarization not only intensifies the feelings of anger and "over-againstness" that characterize life today but also causes them. We are caught in this vicious cycle. People seem to be increasingly fearful, defensive, and aggressive, looking at everything and everyone with suspicion. It is exhausting.

Hostility shapes not just our public discourse but our inner landscape. It creates a state of constant vigilance, where everyone becomes a potential threat rather than a potential friend. This defensive posture exhausts us mentally, emotionally, and spiritually. It narrows our vision, limits our possibilities for connection, and ultimately diminishes our capacity to love.

Hostility comes from a word (*hostis*) that originally meant "stranger" or "enemy." We fear what we do not know or understand. It is so easy to fall into the trap of thinking those who look and think like me are good and those who are different are bad. Nothing is more destructive to the life of love than an "us vs. them mentality." And let us never forget that love casts out fear. The resurgence of a spirit of fear right now is antithetical to a vision of life rooted in love.

In his book *Reaching Out*, Henri Nouwen talks about the need to transform our hostility into hospitality. Love flips our attitude, changing the stranger into a friend or guest. Our words hospital and hospice have the same root as the word hospitality (*hospes*). You care for and about a friend. You want every good thing for them. You offer them the best. You open doors for your friends; you don't slam the door their face. Love in your heart compels you to turn strangers into friends by making room for them in your life and your circle of friends.

When an anti-Muslim spirit seized the hearts of some people in the United States, our daughter, Anna, felt compelled to do something. She had noticed a young Muslim woman about her age at the gym on previous visits and approached her after a workout. "I just wanted to see how you're doing with everything that's happening in the world these days," she said. "I'm sure it's got to be hard and I just want you to know you're not alone. I'm standing with you." The young woman burst into tears. The two fell into a hug and cried together.

That act of kindness broke down the "we/they" barrier and welcomed her into the "one of us" circle. Her new friend's hospitality made her feel welcomed, safe, and loved. Together, they took a leap of faith and committed to growing in a friendship that continues to this day. They decided to bring their Muslim and Christian friends together simply to share a safe space for conversation and connection. An act of kindness and hospitality launched a deep friendship that blossomed into a group they called "Women in Solidarity."

Love transforms strangers into friends. Simple acts pay big dividends. Fear creates division; love leads to unity. You can shape the world around you in this way. When you focus on love rather than fear, doors of opportunity swing open enabling everyone to grow together, understand one another, embrace empathy, and work toward peace. When Anna befriended a stranger at the gym, she probably never dreamed that anything major would come of it. She simply wanted that stranger to know that she had a friend.

The practice of transforming hostility into hospitality requires both inner and outer work. Internally, we must examine our own fears and prejudices, questioning the assumptions that make us quick to categorize others as threats. This inner work creates space for genuine encounter with those who seem different from us.

Externally, we can create environments that nurture connection rather than division. This might mean:

- Making our homes places of welcome where diverse people can gather
- Creating opportunities for meaningful conversation across differences
- Building bridges in our communities through shared meals and celebrations
- Modeling inclusive behavior for our children
- Supporting organizations that bring different groups together

The goal isn't to eliminate all differences—diversity enriches our human family. Rather, the aim is to transform our response to difference from fear to curiosity, from suspicion to openness, from hostility to hospitality.

You are surrounded, literally, with an abundance of potential friends. Some might seem to be just like you. Others are strikingly different. Different clothes, customs, language, skin color. Both are strangers nonetheless. And both may be earnestly longing for a friend. So keep your eyes open for a stranger that might benefit from a kind word, a friendly gesture, and let the wind of love carry you both forward wherever it wants to go.

Transform hostility into hospitality.

Suggested Further Reading:

Yvonne Gentile and Debbie Nixon, *The Art of Hospitality: A Practical Guide for a Ministry of Radical Welcome*, revd edn (Abingdon Press, 2024).

Grace Ji-Sun Kim and Graham Hill, *Healing Our Broken Humanity: Practices for Revitalizing the Church and Renewing the World* (InterVarsity Press, 2018).

Henri J. M. Nouwen, *Reaching Out: The Three Movements of the Spiritual Life* (Image Books, 1986).

Christine Pohl, *Making Room: Recovery Hospitality as a Christian Tradition*, 25th Anniversary Edition (Wm. B. Eerdmans, 2024).

Children's Book: Amy-Jill Levine and Sandy Eisenberg Sasso, *Who Is My Neighbor?* (Flyaway Books, 2019).

Love anyway.

We are called to love everyone. When someone does not reciprocate your love, it is important to continue to show up, pay attention, co-operate with God, and release the outcome. Love anyway in all situations and pray for restoration.

It is easy to love the lovely and the lovable. It is hard to love those who seem to have no interest in returning your love or being kind. What do you do when the love you offer can't or won't be reciprocated? This question haunts just about every family, every workplace, every setting of life today. For those who genuinely seek to love others, this impasse can lead to a kind of catatonic state. You just don't know what to do. This feeling paralyzes, depresses, and can even make you question the possibility, let alone the triumph, of love in our world.

The command to "love anyway" may be the most challenging aspect of love's practice. When someone actively rejects our attempts at connection, when relationship breaks down despite our best efforts, when political or ideological differences create seemingly unbridgeable chasms—these are the moments that test our commitment to love's way. Yet these are precisely the moments when choosing love matters most.

The choice to love anyway doesn't mean accepting abuse or tolerating harm. Instead, it means maintaining

our own capacity for love even when it cannot be reciprocated. It means choosing not to let another's inability
to receive love diminish our ability to offer it. This requires a delicate balance between maintaining appropriate boundaries and keeping our hearts open to the possibility of future connection.

For some these feelings play out around issues of
sexuality, leading to a sense of rejection and abandon-
ment. We all know how political or cultural wedges
divide families and long-term friends in our polarized
world. Factors like drug abuse, alcohol addiction, and
economic hardship can suck love right out of you. This
is real. This is hard. We want to be clear here. If any ver-
bal, physical, sexual, or emotional abuse is involved, it is
okay and necessary to set firm self-protective boundaries
and to seek professional help.

Elaine Heath's four-fold approach to faithful living
applies to non-abusive relationships in which love is lost.
Show up. Pay attention. Co-operate with God. Release
the outcome. In other words, if your love is not being returned it helps no one if you turn a cold shoulder. Keep
your eyes open and try to see what is really going on. Is
there more than meets the eye? Invite God into your di-
lemma. How might God be at work? How can you come
alongside God's efforts to restore love? Pray for the good
of the other. And then, perhaps most importantly, put
everything into God's hands. Relinquish your need to be

the healer. Only the Spirit can do this. And ask God to heal your broken heart if no resolution comes.

Let's explore what each of these elements means in practice:

Showing up means maintaining presence even when it's difficult. This could mean continuing to send birthday cards to an estranged family member, remaining professionally courteous to a hostile colleague, or simply holding space in your heart for someone who has turned away.

Paying attention involves staying alert to subtle shifts and opportunities for connection. Like watching for signs of spring after a long winter, we notice small indications that healing might be possible. This attentiveness helps us respond appropriately when moments of possibility arise.

Co-operating with God reminds us that we're not alone in this work. Sometimes our role is simply to participate in what God is already doing—to be ready to play our part in a larger process of reconciliation and healing that we neither control nor fully understand.

Releasing the outcome may be the most difficult yet liberating aspect. It means trusting that our commitment to love has value regardless of the response it receives. This release frees us from the burden of trying to force particular results and allows us to love more purely.

Janet began a new job in a Christian organization. Most of her co-workers had been in their positions a long time. When asked to lead a devotion at the weekly staff meeting, her pastoral instincts led her to invite her colleagues to share any prayer concerns they might have. She immediately received a cold stare from a woman across the table. "We don't do that here," she sneered. "This isn't church." "I'll never do that again," Janet said to herself. She read her devotion and retreated to her cubicle.

The cold glares continued from this co-worker, so Janet avoided her as much as she could. Simply going to work became stressful. In time, however, she began a discipline of prayer for her co-worker every morning before work. She was always kind, even in the face of provocation. Janet was walking down the hall one day and felt a nudge to stop by this woman's office. She greeted her and asked how her day was going.

To her surprise, the woman burst into tears and began to relate how her mother was dying of cancer. In response, Janet simply listened with empathy and said, "I am so, so sorry." That was a turning point in their relationship and an atmosphere of peace began to prevail, displacing the previous tension. As the adage goes: "Be kind to everyone. You never know what the other person is going through. Love anyway."

Janet's story illustrates a crucial truth about loving anyway: what appears to be rejection often masks deeper pain or fear. Behind cold stares and hostile words, we frequently find wounded hearts longing for connection but afraid to risk it. This doesn't excuse unkind behavior, but understanding it can help us maintain compassion even in difficult relationships.

The practice of loving anyway requires us to develop certain spiritual muscles:

- The patience to wait out seasons of distance

- The humility to keep offering kindness without demanding recognition

- The wisdom to discern between healthy and unhealthy forms of engagement

- The courage to remain vulnerable while maintaining appropriate boundaries

- The faith to trust that love's power extends beyond what we can see

These capabilities don't develop overnight. Like any form of strength, they grow through regular exercise—through daily choices to respond to difficulty with love rather than reactivity.

Animosity. Tension. Division. Unrequited love. Whatever the source of this distress, these things do not disappear miraculously at the drop of a hat. Love demands great patience. But if you continue to show up, pay attention particularly to emotional needs around you, co-operate with God where God is already at work, and place these burdens in God's hands, you might be surprised by what the Spirit of love can do. Remember that you cannot change the other person. Only God can do that. But you do have control over what you do, and kindness is never wrong.

Try to remember that you are not alone in this hard work of love. If you find yourself really grieved by the loss of love in a relationship or a situation, try this. Reach out to a friend that you trust. Share your concern with them. Pray together for a loving outcome. Give thanks to God for the power of love to reconcile and restore. Ask God to help you love anyway, regardless of the response of the other. And whatever happens, know that you have done your very best to love others the way God has loved you.

Suggested Further Reading:

Jeremy Courtney, *Love Anyway: An Invitation Beyond a World that's Scary as Hell* (Zondervan, 2019).

Richard Rohr, *Eager to Love: The Alternative Way of Francis of Assisi* (Franciscan Media, 2024).

Miroslav Volf, *Exclusion and Embrace: A Theological Exploration of Identity, Otherness, and Reconciliation*, revd edn (Abingdon Press, 2019).

Jonathan Wilson-Hartgrove, *Strangers at My Door: A True Story of Finding Jesus in Unexpected Guests* (Convergent Books, 2013).

Children's Book: Alexandra Penfold, *All Are Welcome* (Knopf Books, 2018).

Include the marginalized and stigmatized.

God invites us all to include the marginalized and stigmatized in our circles of love. All your siblings—including the imprisoned and the poor—are people of sacred worth. Solidarity with these beloved of God changes the world.

We have a dear friend, Cari Willis, who inspires us with her unbounded love for the marginalized and stigmatized. She serves as a death row chaplain. Here is a part of her story in her own words:

> When God called me into ministry all I heard was "Go love!" I had no idea that God would be calling me to love those on the row! Thankfully God didn't tell me right off! I don't look up the crimes my friends have allegedly committed. I go to meet a person and not a crime. I go to simply "be" and to "love." I have yet to meet a friend who I haven't loved quite dearly. No one has challenged me in the love department.
>
> The challenge is that the guilty men (half of my friends are innocent), usually have horrific childhood trauma narratives. The trauma starts usually at the age of four and persists into their early teens. So these friends do not know what real love looks like. And some can't trust the love that I have to give because, surely, I will abandon them or just use them.

It takes some friends years before they can trust my love. And so God's love is even more elusive. How does one authentically feel loved by God when they have never been loved their entire lives? It is all a bit too magical and mystical and so therefore cannot be trusted. So I do what I can. I persistently show up for them. I repeatedly tell them, "I love you!"

In Cari's life there is no way to separate the work of love into neat categories like compassion and justice, advocacy and solidarity. These various acts of love blur into a whole way of life as she cares genuinely for those who live in desperation. She models the love of God for those who have never seen it lived out before their eyes.

The profound truth that emerges from Cari's ministry is that inclusion isn't just about making space for others—it's about recognizing that our own humanity is diminished when we exclude. Each act of exclusion, whether personal or systemic, creates ripples of damage that affect both the excluded and those who exclude. Conversely, when we practice radical inclusion, we don't just lift up others—we become more fully human ourselves.

The words *marginalized* and *stigmatized* can sometimes mask the very real human beings they describe. Behind these terms are people with names, stories, dreams, and gifts to share with the world. When we truly understand this, inclusion becomes not just a moral imperative but a recognition that our community is incomplete without each voice, each perspective, each unique contribution.

Marginalization and stigmatization take many forms in our world today. Some politicians exploit these attitudes to acquire more power. They advocate the expansion and implementation of the death penalty. They seek to cage asylum seekers and immigrants. They engage in mass deportation and family separation. They stereotype Muslims as terrorists. They hold the poor in contempt. They sneer at single mothers who provide for their families through federal safety net programs that seek to eliminate poverty. All of this is antithetical to God's way of love. Political action to fight these dehumanizing policies enacts God's love.

The work of inclusion operates on multiple levels simultaneously. While we must address immediate needs—feeding the hungry, sheltering the homeless, visiting the imprisoned—lasting change requires us to examine and transform the systems that create marginalization in the first place. This means:

> Understanding how various forms of exclusion intersect and reinforce each other. Poverty, racism, disability discrimination, and other forms of marginalization often work together to create compound barriers to full participation in community life.

> Recognizing that inclusion isn't about "helping the less fortunate" but about restoring wholeness to

our entire community. When we frame inclusion as charity rather than justice, we perpetuate the very power dynamics that create marginalization.

Some of these issues seem to be insurmountable. They are so immense. They affect so many people who seem to be so far out of reach. Overwhelmed by a sense of powerlessness in the face of evil systems, many simply give up. They close their eyes. Hope things will change. What can one person do? Where do you start? The fact is that you have more power to change the world than you realize. It begins with a change in your heart and small steps you take, one by one.

A friend of ours grew up in Southern Rhodesia, now Zimbabwe. He identified as a white Rhodesian. He had never even visited one person in a Black African homestead in the rural areas just a short drive away. Then a severe drought hit. It did not rain for two years. The deprivation in those farming areas was horrendous. Starvation became the primary cause of death in what were once prosperous communities.

A committed Christian, this friend felt he ought to do something to help. When several people began a drought relief program in the area he got involved. He accompanied his friends on food runs among those who were most needy. For the first time in his life, he stepped foot in the one-room mud huts of his neighbors. The scenes and the people overwhelmed him. He was changed forever and walked through a portal into a new life. He dedicated himself to selfless acts of compassion.

John Wesley provided the following advice to a Methodist woman aspiring to love more fully. It typifies a way of love that seeks to include the marginalized and stigmatized: "Go and see the poor and sick in their own little hovels. Take up your cross, woman! Remember the faith! Jesus went before you, and will go with you. *Put off the gentlewoman: You bear a higher character*" (a letter dated June 9, 1775).

So what can you do to make your world more loving in this regard? Jesus's words in Matthew 25 (CEB) give us a clue:

- "I was hungry and you gave me food": Support Bread for the World (https://www.bread.org/). Cook or serve a meal at a local shelter for people experiencing homelessness. Even better, eat that meal with them.

- "I was thirsty and you gave me a drink": Partner with One Million Wells (https://onemillionwells.org/).

- "I was a stranger and you welcomed me": Connect with a refugee program in your area: (https://give.unrefugees.org/). Volunteer at Family Promise, one of the foremost organizations addressing the crisis of family homelessness, or a local shelter in your community.

- "I was naked and you gave me clothes to wear": De-accumulate and donate clothing to Good Will (https://www.goodwill.org/).
- "I was sick and you took care of me": Call on shut-ins in your faith community.
- "I was in prison and you visited me": Get involved in Prison Fellowship (https://www.prisonfellowship.org/).

Do not attempt all this at once! Simply take a small step in any one of these acts of love that has the power to change the world by including the marginalized and stigmatized.

Suggested Further Reading:

Jenai Auman, *Othered: Finding Belonging with the God Who Pursues the Hurt, Harmed, and Marginalized* (Baker Books, 2024).

Tom Berlin, *Reckless Love: Jesus' Call to Love Our Neighbor* (Abingdon Press, 2019).

Steve Harper, *Holy Love: A Biblical Theology of Human Sexuality* (Abingdon Press, 2019).

bell hooks, *All About Love: New Visions* (William Morrow Publishing, 2018).

Children's Book: Jayneen Sanders, *Included: A book for all children about inclusion, diversity, disability, equality and empathy* (Educate2empower Publishing, 2022).

Simplify that others might simply live.

Consumerism sucks the life out of people and threatens the future of our planet. Faithful living involves a choice between "having," which leads to envy, or "being," which leads to generosity. The simple life is both loving and just.

Money means power all around our globe. It is virtually impossible not be sucked into the culture of consumerism. Having and getting more is so unbelievably seductive. Money gives you the power to consume more goods and services, presumably, those things that make you happy. We are bombarded constantly with the message: consumption will lead to a greater sense of well-being, and we buy the lie. We find ourselves caught in a vicious "work-to-spend" cycle that never ends and, ironically, never delivers.

Do you find yourself trapped in this insidious web? Have you succumbed to the lie? Are you, like so many in our world today, an addictive consumer? Even if trapped, you may yearn to escape this kind of empty and ultimately destructive life? Do you feel compelled to change given the fact that global consumerism is destroying our lives, our communities, and our planet? How does love even speak into this sickness?

The relationship between simplicity and love runs deeper than we often realize. When we're caught in cycles of consumption, our capacity for love becomes constrained in subtle but significant ways. Our attention fragments across our possessions. Our energy depletes in maintaining and managing stuff. Our relationships suffer as we substitute material exchanges for genuine connection. Even our spiritual lives can become commodified, as we seek to purchase rather than practice growth.

The call to simplify isn't about deprivation—it's about liberation. When we begin to disentangle ourselves from the web of consumption, we discover new capacities for presence, attention, and love. Spaces previously filled with things become available for relationships. Time once spent managing possessions becomes free for meaningful connection. Resources previously directed toward accumulation can flow toward genuine needs, both our own and others'.

In the second half of the twentieth century, Erich Fromm published a watershed book entitled *To Have or to Be?* He tackled this issue head on. He understood the personal and social threats associated with this materialist, consumerist way of life. At the time he viewed his book as a manifesto to save our planet from the dangers of rampant consumption. Fromm's basic idea is that two different modes of living compete for your allegiance. He calls one way of life the "having mode." Those who choose this path focus their energy on competition, material possessions, and power. This mode generates greed, envy, and violence.

The other way of life—the "being mode"—is founded upon love, the joy of sharing, and cooperation for the common good. It engenders satisfaction, generosity, and peace. You face the same choice daily between having or being. Are you going to build your life on things that you consume? Or is the call to *be*nlove, to *be* nonviolence, and to *be* in harmony with yourself, others, and our earthly home the desire of your heart?

Francis of Assisi knew something about these two different ways of life centuries ago. When the affluence into which he was born failed to deliver the abundant life, he came to a clear conclusion. He realized that his possessions owned him, and he believed that this did not honor God. So he acted. Many people thought he was crazy. He took his life into his own hands and gave away all that he owned. He decided to embrace a different kind of life. He adopted a simple life after the model of Jesus. He called it a life of "apostolic poverty." Ironically, disentangled from "stuff," for the first time in his life he felt truly free and genuinely happy.

Today, we call this "voluntary simplicity," and while our contemporary practice will differ from Francis's radical renunciations, the underlying principles remain: simplification creates space for love to flourish. This simplification happens in stages, each one opening new possibilities for connection and contribution.

Simplify that others might simply live.

First comes the recognition that our possessions often possess us, demanding our time, attention, and energy in ways that diminish rather than enhance our lives. This awareness itself begins to loosen consumption's grip.

Next comes the intentional process of evaluating what truly adds value to our lives and what merely adds complexity. This isn't about achieving some idealized minimal lifestyle, but about aligning our material lives with our deeper values.

Finally, we discover that simplification isn't just about having less—it's about making room for more of what matters: relationships, creativity, service, and love.

The current "minimalist movement" embraces the same way of life. It is hard to imagine how the problems of poverty will ever be solved if the materially rich and comfortable continue to consume at the rates they do at the expense of the poor. Voluntary simplicity honors and affects your siblings around the world who struggle to survive. It has the power to change this world and make it more loving and just. The goal isn't just individual virtue but collective transformation—creating communities where everyone has enough and no one needs excess to feel secure. This is where simplicity and justice meet, where personal choice becomes social change.

One final thought on this monumental lesson. Simplifying your life impacts the environment directly, and we have no time to waste to save our planet. You can play a role in solving the problem of global warming and climate change. One person can make a huge difference. You are not powerless. Take the simple issue of what you eat as an example. Adopting a more healthy diet is actually a profound expression of love for yourself and our world. A diet of ultra-processed food, meat, and fast food damages your body and our planet more than you might realize. Educate yourself about these issues.

Reducing your meat consumption leads potentially to a reduction of greenhouse gases related to meat production and improves your health. Moving in the direction of a local, whole-food, plant-based lifestyle affirms all living creatures and stands in opposition to animal cruelty and exploitation. Both these actions impact climate change and food security, and lower the probability of suffering and disability related to diabetes, cancer, and heart disease. These may seem like small actions, but they are steps toward a more hopeful future. They are profound acts of restorative love in which simplicity and justice meet.

Practice these daily and at the end of each week take stock of how well you have done and where you can improve in your care of creation:

- Refuse to buy things you do not need.
- Reduce what you feel you must have.
- Reuse everything you possibly can.
- Recycle all items that can be refurbished.
- Return biodegradable items to the earth.

Simplify that others might simply live.

- Reorient to a plant-based diet, even if only one meal per week.
- Rest every week to reduce driving and shopping, and to enjoy God's creation.
- Reform your world through information, advocacy, and political action.
- Restore the planet by walking, cycling, or buying a hybrid or electric car.

These acts of love can change the world and restore creation. Consider how you can be an agent of change by simplifying your life. Consider seriously what your relationship is to money and consumption. Take action to change the orientation of your life from money, things, and more to what really has meaning. Live simply for your sake, for the sake of others, and for the sake of our planet. "'Tis the gift to be simple; 'tis the gift to be free."

Suggested Further Reading:

Erich Fromm, *To Have or to Be?* (Bloomsbury Publishing, 2013).

Jen Hatmaker, *7 Days of Simplicity: A Season of Living Lightly* (Abingdon Press, 2020).

Kate Humble, *A Year of Living Simply: The Joys of a Life Less Complicated* (Aster Publications, 2021).

Richard Rohr, *Simplicity: The Freedom of Letting Go* (Publish-Drive, 2004).

Children's Book: Dr. Seuss, *The Lorax* (Random House, 1971).

Create beauty.

*As human beings we are drawn to beauty. Created in the image
of God, each of us can create—to co-create beauty in the world.
The creation of beauty is an act of love in which
you can engage to light up the world.*

When God began to create" (Gen 1:1 CEB). Love
set everything in motion through a grand, creative
act. The Creator dreamed and drew, sang and sculpted
a universe into being. God combined sound, color, and
shape—the material world in all its diversity and gran-
deur—to establish a home filled with goodness, beauty,
and love. Created in God's image, God breathed into
each of us the ability to create.

This creative capacity isn't a luxury or an add-on to
human nature—it's fundamental to who we are. When
we create beauty, we participate in the ongoing work of
creation itself. Think of how a musician shapes sound
into melody, how a gardener coaxes flowers from soil,
how a cook transforms simple ingredients into a nour-
ishing meal. Each act of creation echoes the first creative
act, bringing something new and beautiful into being.

The connection between beauty and love is profound. Both require attention and care. Both transform
how we see the world and our place in it. Both have

the power to heal and unite. When we create beauty, we aren't just making something pretty—we're participating in love's work of transformation. Whether through art, music, gardening, cooking, writing, or any other creative act, we're saying yes to life's possibility and no to despair's emptiness.

Beauty has a magnetic quality. Who is not drawn to beauty, of whatever form? When you encounter something beautiful doesn't it resonate with something deep inside you? Is there not a connection there? Whenever you perceive beauty, whenever you create beauty, you expand the force of love in the world. The creation of beauty is an act of love, and it is something every human being can do. You can create beauty.

Our world needs beauty desperately. There is so much ugliness and darkness that we fail to see the beauty around us every day. A great pursuer of beauty in the early church by the name of Anselm prayed about this centuries ago. He gives thanks for having been created in God's image so that he can remember, ponder, and love God. But that image, he laments, is so warn and darkened by life that it struggles to reflect the light within.

Leslie Weatherhead was a famous preacher in London during the Second World War. He was noted for his timeless stories drawn from everyday life. According to his son, this was one of his favorites. A little boy grew up in a tiny English village. When he was just the right age, his father took him to London to see all the sites. They packed the day with one adventure after another and returned home exhausted late at night. As his mother tucked her son into bed, she asked him about his favorite part of the day. "We went into this large church," he said. "It had these huge windows filled with people. I've never seen so many different colors in all my life. The thing is, the light shown through those people and made all the place beautiful." You are beautiful, and you have the power to create beauty. What are the creative activities in your life that permit the light to shine through?

Julian Davis Reid, a Black artist-theologian, describes his creative activity as the use of words and music to testify to God's care for our restless world. He invites the weary into the rest of God practiced in the Bible and Black music. We asked him to reflect on his craft. "It can be hard keeping beauty central," he confesses. "Sometimes, especially in jazz, it can be easier to seek competition or achievement more so than beauty. But if I create something beautiful for me, if I remain compelled, then I believe I am establishing a foundation for drawing closer to God." Moreover, he claims that "beauty must open onto service for others. In this sense my desire to create beauty when I play is an attempt at intercession on behalf of the audience." For Julian, the creation of beauty is an act of prayer.

Don't you enjoy creating something beautiful or participating in some activity that fills the world with beauty? Give any child a box of crayons and they will immediately begin to create a masterpiece. Join in coloring with your child and see if you don't experience the joy of your inner child. Joy and healing come with painting and sculpting and singing and writing and building— any form of art, any creative endeavor. The sky is the limit to your creative power.

Art therapy draws upon the healing power of the creative arts. Art therapists help people of all ages explore, release, and share their innermost feelings and experiences, telling their own unique stories in a safe space of healing and love. One of our daughters, Rebekah, is a licensed professional counselor and art therapist. She describes the connections between therapeutic art and beauty:

> Art therapy helps people who are experiencing grief and trauma get pain out of their body and onto paper. Through this empowering experience they can begin to understand what they have been through and heal. This process and the images that emerge often become a powerful catalyst for beauty and positive change, both in the individuals themselves and in the world.

When you create something beautiful—particularly when you draw from the depth of your being—you tap into the source of beauty and let it flow into material forms that you yourself and others can enjoy. That beauty stirs wonder and awe. It provides an opportunity for you and others to ponder and gaze on an object or listen to a sound that is bigger than you are. All great art beckons you to come, wonder, and celebrate beauty in community.

Most of us think of art as an individual pursuit. The idea that beauty must "open onto service" challenges our often individualistic notion of creativity. It suggests that the creation of beauty isn't just about personal expression but about contribution to community. This understanding transforms how we think about creative acts: A grandmother teaching her grandchild to bake isn't just passing on recipes—she's creating a beautiful moment of connection that serves both present and future. A neighborhood mural project doesn't just brighten a wall—it creates a space of shared pride and belonging. A choir singing together isn't just making music—they're weaving a tapestry of harmony that serves both performers and listeners.

On a visit to a nursing home one Christmas season, we had a youth who took his violin with hopes of playing "Silent Night" for the residents. Talking with the staff, we discovered that one of the residents, a ninety-year-old stroke victim, was an accomplished violinist. Due to physical impairment from a stroke, however, he could no longer play his instrument, a deep grief to him. This sensitive teen quietly asked the man if he wanted to play his violin with him. With his arm around his shoulder, this young man fingered as the elderly musician drew the bow across the strings with his functional arm. It took both to make something beautiful. What a parable.

Julia Cameron, in her book *The Artist's Way*, describes a practice that helps unlock the artist within. She calls this Morning Pages. In a similar vein, we invite you to invest some time in what we will call a Weekly Creative Adventure. Set aside a block of time most convenient for you once a week. Find a quiet and comfortable space free of distractions. Gather some materials together—any materials. Whatever strikes your fancy. Invite others to join the activity. Then draw, color, sculpt, compose, sing, play. Play, and enjoy. Just let something beautiful flow out of you. Reflect on the experience. Display your treasure in your home or share what you have created with others.

Each week, seek to create something beautiful. Let the light shine through. Fill the world with beauty and love.

Suggested Further Reading:

Jeremy S. Begbie, *Abundantly More: The Theological Promise of the Arts in a Reductionist World* (Baker Books, 2023).

Create beauty.

Julia Cameron, *The Artist's Way: A Spiritual Path to Higher Creativity* (TarcherPerigee, 2016)

Thomas Dubay, *The Evidential Power of Beauty: Science and Theology Meet* (Ignatius Press, 1999).

Makoto Fujimura, *Culture Care: Reconnecting with Beauty for Our Common Life* (InterVarsity Press, 2017).

Children's Book: Barney Saltzberg, *Beautiful Oops!* (Workman Pub. Co., 2010).

Promote peace with justice.

Our world needs peace now more than ever. Peace is much more than the absence of conflict or war. It consists of wellness, wholeness, and justice for all people. Your actions can lead to a time in which peace with justice prevails.

Sometimes it seems like the prophet Jeremiah just read your newsfeed from the morning.

> From the least to the greatest of them, everyone is greedy for unjust gain; and from prophet to priest, everyone deals falsely. They have treated the wound of my people carelessly, saying, "Peace, peace," where there is no peace. (6:13-14 NRSVUE)

Peace is so elusive. Polarization tears apart communities and families. Divisions are endemic. War leaves hundreds of thousands devastated and kills so many innocent children in our human family. Age-old fault lines of hate threaten to fracture our fragile world. We cry out, "Peace, peace." But there is no peace. Where in the world do you even start?

This topic is so huge that it is hard to know, in fact, where to begin. But all peace—whether on the level of personal relationships or in the sphere of international conflict—begins in human hearts. Howard Thurman describes the "citadel of the heart" as that place where you nurture all your loves and all your hates, all your hopes and all your fears. *The Anatomy of Peace* by The Arbinger Institute explores the complexity of peace as it relates to the heart. It invites you to ask the question, do I have a heart of conflict or a heart of peace?

Peace depends on the power of love to transform the heart. It requires deep self-examination. The drive to justify your own attitudes and actions easily leads you to see others as obstacles instead of people. One of the greatest barriers to peace is the desire to win and for someone else to lose. On the other hand, the quest for peace also requires profound empathy. When other people direct their anger and aggression towards you, it may be coming from a place of misdirected pain. Peace depends on your ability to see others as wounded human beings, potential friends who deserve your good will. We like to remind ourselves often that when we sing "Come into my heart, Lord Jesus," he always says, "Only if I can bring my friends." Peace comes when you invite them in.

The most profound biblical term for peace is the Hebrew word *shalom*. Often simply translated peace, it means so much more. It connotes a comprehensive wellness and wholeness, beginning with individuals and extending outward to the entire cosmos. Shalom is more than the absence of conflict or war. It refers to the restoration of peace with justice in the lives of all people. There can be no peace without justice; justice is the soil in which you plant the seeds of peace. Being a peacemaker means partnering with God in the restoration of goodness, beauty, and love. Peace is possible.

In these few pages it would be presumptuous of us to offer advice concerning peace in the global sphere. But we do need to ask some questions closer to home. Does your heart or your home ever feel like a battlefield? Has conflict become a normalized part of your life like an unwelcome house guest who refuses to leave? Has tension and anxiety increased recently? If you feel the way we do about life right now, we fear it has. The spirit of this age seeps into the most intimate spaces of our lives these days.

One of our favorite lines of all time from a romantic comedy comes from *While You Were Sleeping*. Jack has something important to share with his dad. He's a bit anxious because it's potentially unsettling news. But before Jack has a chance to share his concern, his father talks wistfully about his desire for a moment's peace. He longs for just one minute when everyone is healthy, everyone is happy, and life is good for everyone. Jack responds with this simple reply, "Hey Pop, this is not that minute." Have you felt like that? We have, frequently. Does it seem to you like that minute of peace will never come?

You find yourself dealing every day with "the ordinary mess." Here, perhaps more than anywhere else, we don't want to rush in with grand strategies for changing the world. You must approach the quest for peace with humility, but also with a firm confidence. Since all peace begins in the heart, why not develop a place of peace in your home that can become a focal point for all your peacemaking activities? We suggest that you create a "peace corner." Include calming elements like a candle or plant. Explore and collect opportunities for peacemaking in your community and beyond, thereby developing a library of projects for peace.

Building peace with justice is like tending a garden that spans from our doorstep to the horizon. In our immediate vicinity—our personal relationships and daily interactions—we cultivate peace through intimate, hands-on work. Here, we learn to resolve conflicts in ways that deepen rather than damage relationships. We practice speaking truth with love rather than wielding it as a weapon. We create small spaces of dialogue where understanding can grow across differences. When we cause harm, we learn the humble work of making amends. These personal practices might seem small, but like well-tended garden beds, they create fertile soil where peace can take root.

Moving beyond our personal sphere, we find ourselves working in the community garden of peace. Here, the work becomes more complex, requiring collaboration with others who bring different tools and techniques to the task. We support initiatives that bring diverse groups together, much like planting complementary species that help each other thrive. We look beneath surface conflicts to address root causes, just as a gardener must understand soil conditions to grow healthy plants. We build structures that ensure everyone has access to the garden's bounty, creating systems for equitable participation and shared decision-making.

But our garden of peace extends even further, into the broader landscape of systemic change. Here, we're no longer just tending individual plants or even community gardens—we're working to transform the entire ecosystem. This means addressing structural inequalities that make peaceful solutions difficult to sustain. It involves supporting nonviolent movements for change, much like establishing wildlife corridors that allow natural systems to heal and reconnect. We develop alternatives to violence, building networks of mutual support that can weather storms and seasons of challenge.

These levels of peacework aren't separate—they're deeply interconnected, like the layers of a healthy ecosystem. The peace we cultivate in our personal relationships nourishes our capacity for community engagement. The trust and understanding built through community peacebuilding create fertile ground for systemic change. And when we succeed in transforming unjust systems, we make it easier for peace to flourish at every level.

Remember to use your voice. You can make a difference as you encourage elected officials to pursue peaceful diplomatic and economic development. These are the true foundations of all lasting peace. Threats, violence, and military might lead to deeper trauma; development is an act of love that fosters peace. Choose a particular

focus for your personal attention every three months—
personal, local, or global—however the Spirit leads. Ask
yourself the simple question, what practical action can I
take regarding this area of peacemaking that cultivates
a heart of peace and opens a wider space for love and
justice in the world?

What barrier to peace is there, in fact, that love cannot break? Acts of love pave the way for peace with justice. Love never takes, it always gives. Love never resents,
it always delights. The power of love endures; the power
of fear implodes. A heart of conflict harms; a heart of
peace heals. We long for the day the power of love prevails over the love of power. On that day, the world—
and you—will know peace.

Suggested Further Reading:

The Arbinger Institute, *The Anatomy of Peace: Resolving the
Heart of Conflict*, 4th edn (Berrett-Koehler, 2022).

Walter Brueggemann, *Living Toward a Vision: Biblical Reflections on Shalom* (United Church Press, 1976).

John Paul Lederach, *The Moral Imagination: The Art and Soul of
Building Peace* (Oxford University Press, 2020).

Lisa Schirch, *The Little Book of Strategic Peacebuilding: A Vision
and Framework for Peace with Justice* (Good Books, 2005).

Children's Book: Julie D. Penshorn, *I Can See Peace* (Growing
Communities for Peace, 2018).

Plant seeds of hope.

Love is intimately connected with hope. In a world of hopelessness, planting seeds of hope is an essential act of love. Whenever you restore hope in someone's life, this fosters beloved community —a more loving and just world.

It is impossible to love if you have no hope. Hope and love go hand in hand. Similarly, hopelessness and helplessness are intertwined. The absence of hope leads to a deep sense of loneliness and helplessness. If hope is about something you cannot see, then all the hopeless situations that you do see or experience yourself make it so hard to hope for a loving future. At a time when many seem to be hopeless, it is important to think about the connection between hope and love.

Hope isn't just optimism or positive thinking—it's an active force that shapes how we engage with the world. When we plant seeds of hope, we're not simply waiting passively for things to get better. We're participating in love's transformative work, creating conditions where new possibilities can take root and grow. Like a gardener who plants in faith that spring will come, we act in the present based on our trust in future flourishing.

The metaphor of seed-planting is particularly apt because it acknowledges both the smallness of our individual actions and their potential for exponential growth. Every great forest began with single seeds. Every movement for positive change started with small acts of hope. When we understand this, we see that no act of love is too small to matter. Each loving action plants a seed that carries within it the possibility of transformation.

Reflect for a moment about a time when you were hopeless. Perhaps you feel hopeless at this very moment. If something restored your hope in the past, how did that happen? Was it an act you witnessed? A kind word spoken to you at the right time? Did you begin the day depressed and weary only to find yourself uplifted and eager to engage life anew by the end of the day? Hope is extremely fragile. It can be easily lost, but hope can also be restored in the twinkling of an eye. Wherever hope is rekindled, it makes love possible.

Jürgen Moltmann will go down in history as the father of the "theology of hope." During one of his visits to Duke University, Paul invited him to lunch. While introducing himself more fully, Paul explained that he was working in his doctoral studies with Frank Baker. "Oh," Moltmann interrupted, "Would you like to hear a story about Frank and Nellie Baker?" Paul sat back to take it all in.

> During World War II there was a German prison of war camp on the northeast coast of England near the city of Hull. A young pastor and his wife served a small

Methodist circuit close by. They were filled with com-passion and compelled to do something to reach out to the German prisoners who were their neighbors. They went to the commander and asked permission to take a prisoner with them to church each Sunday and then to their home where they would eat their Sunday dinner together. It was agreed. So Sunday after Sunday, a steady flow of German soldiers worshiped and ate with the Bakers in their home throughout the course of the war.

This world-famous theologian paused, looked at Paul intently, and said, "One of those soldiers was a young man by the name of Jürgen Moltmann, and it was at Frank and Nellie Baker's dinner table that the seed of hope was planted in my heart."

The Bakers couldn't have known that their Sunday hospitality would help shape one of the twentieth cen-tury's most influential theologians. They simply opened their home and their hearts, planting seeds of hope through regular acts of inclusion and care.

Their example teaches us several crucial lessons about hope. First, that hope often grows best in the soil of relationship. The Bakers didn't just feed bodies; they nourished souls through genuine connection and com-munity. Second, that hope requires courage—the cour-age to cross boundaries, to welcome strangers, to love in spite of social pressure or potential criticism. Third, that hope's impact often extends far beyond what we can see. The seeds we plant may bear fruit in ways we never witness, in lives we never know we've touched.

In rural Rwanda, Marie Claire, herself orphaned as a young teen, adopted her four young nieces and nephews to keep them from becoming "street kids." She described their life as very hard, saying, "I was a child too, and needed parents, but we had not anyone." They were isolated, often hungry, and unable to go to school. They had no hope for a better life. Zoe Empowers staff found her and invited her to join an empowerment group. She was encouraged to dream dreams again. She dreamed of becoming a tailor, having a sewing machine, and owning chickens. Through her first small Zoe grant, she began selling chickens and rabbits. She saved her profits and sent her nieces and nephews back to school. She learned tailoring from her mentor and bought her own sewing machine. Now they all are thriving, helping other children, and working hard towards their next dream of owning a home.

You can love others by planting seeds of hope in their lives. Fill your days with hope-building acts of love. Consider supporting Zoe Empowers (https://zoeempowers.org). Make it a long-term commitment that restores hope, life, and love in God's beloved children. Through Zoe you can equip vulnerable youth with solutions to overcome extreme poverty—for good—and enable desperate families to flourish. Through an act like this, you can practice love on the most basic of levels, and small gifts make a huge impact. Your action can literally save the lives of fellow human beings who have names. And whenever your action saves a life, your embodiment of love reverberates throughout the world. The universe is forever changed.

Suggested Further Reading:

Paul W. Chilcote and Steve Harper, *Living Hope: An Inclusive Vision of the Future* (Cascade Books, 2020).

Cynthia Ruchti, *A Fragile Hope* (Abingdon Press, 2017).

Melissa Spoelstra, *Dare to Hope: Living Intentionally in an Unstable World* (Abingdon Press, 2019).

Laceye C. Warner and Gaston Warner, *From Relief to Empowerment: How Your Church Can Cultivate Sustainable Mission* (Foundery Books, 2017).

Children's Book: Amy Parker, *How High Is Hope?* (B&H Kids, 2016).

Trust God
no matter what.

*God's steadfast love endures forever. All day long God is at work
for good in the world. God seeks to restore goodness, beauty, and
love in everything. You are God's beloved child.
Let this be your anchor.*

Epilogue
Love in Action Tomorrow

Experience has taught us that intentionality plays a major role in your ability to love. Love is a decision as much as a feeling. Feelings come and go, but genuine love has a certain kind of permanence that anchors your life. Having concluded this little book of lessons, we hope that you feel more anchored in love. Perhaps even more importantly, we hope that you feel that you can make a difference. You can make this world a more loving and just place.

The relational character of love means that it can only be experienced and expressed with others. A life of love is not a solo marathon with the goal of a perfect finish. It's not even a relay race in which you hand off the baton of love to the next in line. No. The life of love is more like a family—a community—aiming in the same direction. The goal toward which we all move together is the fullest possible restoration of goodness, beauty, and love. Given the fact that those three qualities in life are larger than any of us, the end toward which we strive is more like a flying goal. It is always before us, ahead of us. At the same time, however, every act of love moves us upward and outward.

You may have made the decision at the outset to read this book with others. Fantastic, if that is the case. We hope that everything you have shared in the journey continues to lift you up, challenges you toward next steps, and fills you with joy. If this was a solo venture for you, consider another run through these lessons with others close to you in life, or with a group of people you long to know better. The life of love is an adventure meant to be shared.

Love, we believe, also requires accountability. That is part of the intentionality related to the life of love. You have made a start. What is your plan to carry this forward as you seek to love more fully, to grow in that love? Undoubtedly, as you put your love into practice in response to each of the lessons, some loving actions came quite naturally, while others pushed the envelope for you. Obviously, you cannot do all these practices at the same time. You would have no time to live. But which practices proved more helpful to you? Where did your growth in love take place? What are your strengths and your weaknesses in the way of love? While everyone of us remains a novice in love, what do you feel called to master? What new horizons have emerged that you want to pursue?

A cadre of companions helps make all these questions real. Fellowship with others grounds your own journey. Friends help keep your feet on the ground. They help you to keep it real. Moreover, others can often see things in you that you cannot see in yourself. That can be both positive and negative, but on either side of that equation it is all good. Growth only happens when you confront the real you with the realities of your life.

A dear friend once told us that each of us is composed of three selves. We display the external self as actors who want to be seen by others in a particular way. This involves masks. The present self represents the real you, just as you are now, warts and all. But each of us, hopefully, stretches forward toward our true self. That true self is the fully loving you. Do you have a better vision of who that is? Have your companions helped you discover that truly loving human being hidden deep inside and longing to break out? What an adventure! What an amazing journey! You are created for love!

In your quest to make this world a better place through your acts of love, be kind to yourself. Don't beat yourself up when you fail to love as you would wish. All of us fail in this way. We often struggle to love others and ourselves. In those moments, acknowledge the reality of it all, embrace your deepest longings, and simply try to do better. On the other hand, when you see how your acts of love have changed other people's lives for the better, celebrate, not yourself, but love itself. Because that love has drawn you closer to someone, no doubt. That love has opened doors for others that they hardly

dreamed were possible. That love has released affirmation, and acceptance, and abundance into the world.
You have been an instrument of love, and the world is
forever changed for the better because of your courage.

In her poem "Touched by an Angel," Maya Angelou
affirms that love breaks the chains of our fear. She cele-
brates the way the light of love elicits bravery, concluding
with these memorable lines:

> Yet it is only love
> which sets us free.